Illegal Immigration

Other Books in the Current Controversies Series

Illegal Immigration

Noël Merino, Book Editor

GREENHAVEN PRESS
A part of Gale, Cengage Learning

Detroit • New York • San Francisco • New Haven, Conn • Waterville, Maine • London

Elizabeth Des Chenes, *Managing Editor*

© 2012 Greenhaven Press, a part of Gale, Cengage Learning

Gale and Greenhaven Press are registered trademarks used herein under license.

For more information, contact:
Greenhaven Press
27500 Drake Rd.
Farmington Hills, MI 48331-3535
Or you can visit our Internet site at gale.cengage.com

For product information and technology assistance, contact us at

Gale Customer Support, 1-800-877-4253
For permission to use material from this text or product, submit all requests online at www.cengage.com/permissions

Further permissions questions can be emailed to permissionrequest@cengage.com

Articles in Greenhaven Press anthologies are often edited for length to meet page requirements. In addition, original titles of these works are changed to clearly present the main thesis and to explicitly indicate the author's opinion. Every effort is made to ensure that Greenhaven Press accurately reflects the original intent of the authors. Every effort has been made to trace the owners of copyrighted material.

Cover image Kellie L. Folkerts/Shutterstock.com

LIBRARY OF CONGRESS CATALOGING-IN-PUBLICATION DATA

Illegal immigration / Noël Merino, book editor.
  p. cm. -- (Current controversies)
  Includes bibliographical references and index.
  ISBN 978-0-7377-5624-1 (hardcover) -- ISBN 978-0-7377-5625-8 (pbk.)
  1. Illegal aliens--United States. 2. United States--Emigration and immigration--Government policy. I. Merino, Noël.
  JV6483.I524 2011
  325.73--dc22

                                                      2011014482

Printed in the United States of America
1 2 3 4 5 6 7 15 14 13 12 11

Contents

Chapter 1: Is There an Illegal Immigration Crisis in the United States?

Yes: There Is an Illegal Immigration Crisis in the United States

No: There Is Not an Illegal Immigration Crisis in the United States

Chapter 2: Does Illegal Immigration Harm US Citizens?

Yes: Illegal Immigration Harms US Citizens

Millions of Americans are unemployed as a result of illegal immigrants doing jobs that could be done by Americans if immigration laws were enforced.

No: Illegal Immigration Does Not Harm US Citizens

Chapter 3: Are Current Policies Regarding Illegal Immigrants Working?

Yes: Current Policies Regarding Illegal Immigrants Are Working

Chapter 4: How Should the Government Respond to Illegal Immigration?

Foreword

By definition, controversies are "discussions of questions in which opposing opinions clash" (Webster's Twentieth Century Dictionary Unabridged). Few would deny that controversies are a pervasive part of the human condition and exist on virtually every level of human enterprise. Controversies transpire between individuals and among groups, within nations and between nations. Controversies supply the grist necessary for progress by providing challenges and challengers to the status quo. They also create atmospheres where strife and warfare can flourish. A world without controversies would be a peaceful world; but it also would be, by and large, static and prosaic.

The Series' Purpose

The purpose of the Current Controversies series is to explore many of the social, political, and economic controversies dominating the national and international scenes today. Titles selected for inclusion in the series are highly focused and specific. For example, from the larger category of criminal justice, Current Controversies deals with specific topics such as police brutality, gun control, white collar crime, and others. The debates in Current Controversies also are presented in a useful, timeless fashion. Articles and book excerpts included in each title are selected if they contribute valuable, long-range ideas to the overall debate. And wherever possible, current information is enhanced with historical documents and other relevant materials. Thus, while individual titles are current in focus, every effort is made to ensure that they will not become quickly outdated. Books in the Current Controversies series will remain important resources for librarians, teachers, and students for many years.

In addition to keeping the titles focused and specific, great care is taken in the editorial format of each book in the series. Book introductions and chapter prefaces are offered to provide background material for readers. Chapters are organized around several key questions that are answered with diverse opinions representing all points on the political spectrum. Materials in each chapter include opinions in which authors clearly disagree as well as alternative opinions in which authors may agree on a broader issue but disagree on the possible solutions. In this way, the content of each volume in Current Controversies mirrors the mosaic of opinions encountered in society. Readers will quickly realize that there are many viable answers to these complex issues. By questioning each author's conclusions, students and casual readers can begin to develop the critical thinking skills so important to evaluating opinionated material.

Current Controversies is also ideal for controlled research. Each anthology in the series is composed of primary sources taken from a wide gamut of informational categories including periodicals, newspapers, books, US and foreign government documents, and the publications of private and public organizations. Readers will find factual support for reports, debates, and research papers covering all areas of important issues. In addition, an annotated table of contents, an index, a book and periodical bibliography, and a list of organizations to contact are included in each book to expedite further research.

Perhaps more than ever before in history, people are confronted with diverse and contradictory information. During the Persian Gulf War, for example, the public was not only treated to minute-to-minute coverage of the war, it was also inundated with critiques of the coverage and countless analyses of the factors motivating US involvement. Being able to sort through the plethora of opinions accompanying today's major issues, and to draw one's own conclusions, can be a complicated and frustrating struggle. It is the editors' hope that Current Controversies will help readers with this struggle.

Introduction

"Arizona's Support Our Law Enforcement
and Safe Neighborhoods Act has been a
source of controversy since it was signed
into law on April 23, 2010."

In a 2010 publication, the US Department of Homeland Security estimates that there are more than 10 million unauthorized, or illegal, immigrants in the United States. Illegal immigrants may enter the United States unlawfully, or may be admitted on a temporary basis and stay past the date they are required to leave. The vast majority of the unauthorized immigrant population is from Mexico. Within the United States, illegal immigrants reside in states bordering Mexico in disproportionate numbers. California is home to almost a quarter of the undocumented immigrants, and Texas is home to more than 15 percent of illegal immigrants. The US-Mexican border runs approximately 350 miles along the south of Arizona, and Arizona is home to almost half a million unauthorized immigrants, with many illegal immigrants crossing its border illegally to gain entry to the United States before heading elsewhere. In response to concern about illegal immigration, in 2010 Arizona passed the controversial Support Our Law Enforcement and Safe Neighborhoods Act, otherwise known as Arizona Senate Bill 1070.

The Arizona act attempts to increase enforcement of federal immigration laws by directing Arizona law enforcement officers to check immigration status during the course of any lawful stop, detention, or arrest where "reasonable suspicion exists that the person is an alien and is unlawfully present in the United States." Individuals are presumed to not be illegal immigrants if they provide a valid Arizona driver's license or identification license, tribal identification, or government-issued identification. If a law enforcement agency determines that an individual convicted of a violation of state or local law is in the country illegally, the act demands that the United States Immigration and Customs Enforcement (ICE) or the United States Customs and Border Protection be notified. Even without conviction, the act allows law enforcement to obtain judicial authorization to transfer an illegal immigrant to federal custody. The act also allows a law enforcement officer to arrest a person without a warrant if the officer has probable cause that the person has committed an offense that warrants removal from the United States.

The act makes it a state misdemeanor for illegal immigrants to fail to carry documentation of alien status required by federal law, allowing undocumented illegal immigrants to be arrested by local law enforcement in Arizona. In addition, the act forbids state agencies from adopting laws and policies that are in conflict with federal immigration law and allows legal residents to sue state or localities that restrict enforcement of federal law. The act also makes it unlawful to hire an unauthorized immigrant for work and to transport an illegal immigrant.

Arizona's Support Our Law Enforcement and Safe Neighborhoods Act has been a source of controversy since it was signed into law on April 23, 2010. In an April 2010 Gallup poll, 39 percent of Americans favored the Arizona law, 30 percent opposed it, and 31 percent had not heard of it or had no opinion. Arizona governor Jan Brewer said at the signing of the bill that the act "represents another tool for our state to use as we work to solve a crisis we did not create and the federal government has refused to fix." In an April 2010 article by Randal C. Archibold in the *New York Times*, President Barack Obama criticized the law, claiming that it threatened "to undermine basic notions of fairness that we cherish as Americans, as well as the trust between police and our communities that is so crucial to keeping us safe." In an article on

CNN.com, Governor Brewer claimed, "As committed as I am to protecting our state from crime associated with illegal immigration I am equally committed to holding law enforcement accountable should this statute ever be misused to violate an individual's rights."

Several lawsuits have been filed against Arizona, including one by the US Justice Department, challenging the law for usurping federal responsibility for control of immigration. On July 28, 2010, US district court judge Susan Bolton issued a ruling on the Justice Department's lawsuit, blocking the most controversial aspects of Arizona's Support Our Law Enforcement and Safe Neighborhoods Act just one day before the law was to go into effect. Among the blocked portions is the requirement that law enforcement officials check immigration status, which Judge Bolton claimed would overwhelm the federal immigration system and result in people being wrongly detained. She also barred the component of the act that allowed a law enforcement officer to arrest a person without a warrant and the section that made it a state crime to fail to carry alien registration documents. Arizona is fighting the ruling, and as of early 2011 the case was still working its way through the legal system. Governor Brewer has said the state would file a countersuit against the federal government for not enforcing federal immigration laws.

Other states are keeping a close eye on Arizona to see what happens. Although immigration has historically been considered an issue of federal jurisdiction, many states are frustrated by what they see as the failure of federal immigration policy. The issue of illegal immigration has long created controversy. Strong disagreement can be found, to begin, on the issue of whether or not illegal immigration is a problem, and whether or not the existence of illegal immigrants harms Americans. It is not hard to find strong critics of current immigration policies, but even among the critics a lack of consensus exists concerning just what policies the government should implement in response to illegal immigration. These contentious issues, which are unlikely to be resolved in the near future, are explored and debated in *Current Controversies: Illegal Immigration.*

CHAPTER 1

Is There an Illegal Immigration Crisis in the United States?

Overview: Unauthorized Immigration in the United States

Jeffrey S. Passel and D'Vera Cohn

Jeffrey S. Passel is senior demographer and D'Vera Cohn a senior writer at the Pew Hispanic Center, a nonpartisan research organization and project of the Pew Research Center.

As of March 2009, 11.1 million unauthorized immigrants were living in the United States. Pew Hispanic Center estimates indicate that the size of the unauthorized immigrant population peaked in 2007 at 12 million. From 2007 to 2009, the number of unauthorized immigrants declined by a million people, or 8%.

The Estimated Unauthorized Immigrant Population

This decline represents a change in the pattern throughout the decade. There were 8.4 million unauthorized immigrants in 2000, a number that increased in 2001, leveled off for two years and then grew steadily from 2003 to 2007. Despite the population's recent decline, the number of unauthorized immigrants grew 32% from 2000 to 2009.

The number of unauthorized immigrants in 2008, 11.6 million, appears to be larger than the number in 2009, but this finding is inconclusive because the difference between estimates for the two years is not statistically significant. The estimates are derived from sample surveys and thus are subject to uncertainty from sampling error, as well as other types of error. Each annual estimate of the unauthorized population is actually the midpoint of a range of possible values that could be the true number. In addition, the change has its own margin of error.

These ranges represent 90% confidence intervals, meaning that there is a 90% probability that the interval contains the true value. . . .

Despite the population's recent decline, the number of unauthorized immigrants grew 32% from 2000 to 2009.

According to estimates from the Department of Homeland Security [DHS], 10.8 million unauthorized immigrants were living in the United States in January 2009, compared with 11.8 million in 2007, the peak number for the decade. These estimates are consistent with the Pew Hispanic Center estimates. The DHS estimates were developed using a similar methodology but were based on a different Census Bureau data source, the American Community Survey.

Foreign-Born Population Trends

Of the nation's 39.4 million foreign-born residents in 2009, 72%, or 28.4 million, were legal immigrants in one of three main categories: 14.6 million naturalized citizens, 12.4 million legal permanent residents and 1.4 million legal temporary migrants.[1]

The annual net average growth of the unauthorized immigrant population declined notably over the decade. By contrast, the flow of legal immigrants increased slightly. As documented in a 2008 Pew Hispanic Center report, the annual flows of legal residents began to surpass the annual flows of unauthorized residents around 2007, reversing a trend that began in the late 1990s.

The combination of decreased flow of unauthorized immigrants and slightly increased flow of legal immigrants has

---

1. Because of rounding, numbers throughout the report may not sum to the total.

played a role in changing the composition of the nation's foreign-born population. Unauthorized immigrants have become a smaller share of the nation's foreign-born population: 28% in 2009, compared with 31% in 2007.

State Settlement Patterns

In concert with the national decrease in unauthorized immigration, some south Atlantic and mountain states experienced statistically significant declines in their unauthorized immigrant populations from 2008 to 2009. No state had a statistically significant increase.

The south Atlantic division, which extends between Delaware and Florida and includes several states that have become new immigrant magnets in recent years, had a decline in its unauthorized population, from 2.5 million in 2008 to 2 million in 2009.

Within that division, Florida's unauthorized immigrant population declined by 375,000 during that one-year period, to an estimated 675,000 people. The number of unauthorized immigrants in Virginia declined by 65,000, to 240,000 people. In the area that encompasses the rest of the region, the unauthorized immigrant population declined by 160,000, to 1 million.

Among the mountain states as a group,[2] the number of unauthorized immigrants declined by 160,000, to 1 million, from 2008 to 2009. Nevada was the only state to have its own statistically significant decline; its unauthorized immigrant population went down by 50,000 during that year, to an estimated 180,000. A group of three other mountain states— Arizona, Colorado and Utah—had a combined decline of 130,000 unauthorized immigrants, to a 2009 total of 700,000.

2. The mountain states are Arizona, Colorado, Idaho, Montana, Nevada, New Mexico, Utah, and Wyoming.

States with the Most
Unauthorized Immigrants

Although unauthorized immigrants live in every state, they are highly concentrated in only a few states. In 2009, just over half (54%) lived in only five states that are longtime immigrant destinations—California, Texas, Florida, New York and Illinois. California alone houses nearly a quarter (23%) of the nation's unauthorized immigrants.

States with large numbers of unauthorized immigrants also include several that have become new destinations over the past two decades. They include Georgia, Arizona and North Carolina, where more than a million were estimated to reside in 2009. Those states' combined share of the unauthorized immigrant population grew to 10% in 2009 from 4% in 1990.

Unauthorized immigrants accounted for 3.7% of the nation's population in 2009. Their shares of states' total population were highest in California (6.9%), Nevada (6.8%) and Texas (6.5%). Arizona (5.8%) and New Jersey (5.6%) round out the top five states where unauthorized immigrants made up the largest share of the population in 2009.

Latin American countries account for the overwhelming majority—four-in-five—of unauthorized immigrants.

There also are seven states—Alaska, Maine, Montana, North Dakota, South Dakota, Vermont and West Virginia—where unauthorized immigrants account for less than 1% of the population; the Pew Hispanic Center estimates that the unauthorized immigrant population in each of those states was less than 10,000 in 2009.

Country of Origin of
Unauthorized Immigrants

Latin American countries account for the overwhelming majority—four-in-five—of unauthorized immigrants. In March

2009, there were 8.9 million unauthorized immigrants in the U.S. from Mexico and other parts of Latin America. Of those, 6.7 million were from Mexico, or 60% of all unauthorized immigrants. An additional 2.2 million unauthorized immigrants, or 20% of the total, were from other Latin American nations (about 1.3 million from Central America, 575,000 from South America and 350,000 from the Caribbean).

Unauthorized immigrants from South and East Asia accounted for 1.2 million of the total, or 11%; Europe and Canada accounted for about 475,000 unauthorized immigrants, or 4%. Smaller numbers came from the Middle East (150,000, or about 1% of the total).

The unauthorized population from Mexico grew steadily from 2001 through 2007, expanding from 4.8 million to 7 million during those years. Since then, the number from Mexico has been stable.

The population of unauthorized immigrants from other countries in Latin America did not grow at a statistically significant rate until it peaked at 2.8 million in 2006. After holding steady in 2007, the numbers dropped notably—to 2.2 million in 2009. That represents a decline of 22% over the two-year period.

The number of unauthorized immigrants from other nations grew in 2001 but was statistically unchanged after that. In 2009, 2.2 million unauthorized immigrants came from nations outside Latin America. That represents a 20% share of unauthorized immigrants in 2009.

Over the decade, the share of unauthorized immigrants who are from Mexico rose from 51% in 2001[3] to 60% in 2009. The share from other Latin American nations declined from 25% in 2001 to 20% in 2009. The share from nations outside Latin America decreased slightly, from 24% in 2001 to 20% in 2009.

3. National and state population estimates for 2000 are based on Census 2000; all other estimates of the population and its characteristics are based on the Current Population Survey. Therefore, totals may differ slightly.

About three-quarters of unauthorized immigrants are Hispanic (76%); among non-Hispanics, 11% are Asian, 8% are white and 5% are black.

The Unabated Flow of Illegal Immigrants Must Be Stopped

Donald Mann

Donald Mann is president of Negative Population Growth, a membership organization founded to educate the American public about the detrimental effects of overpopulation.

W hat measures are needed to halt illegal immigration and compel settled illegal aliens to leave the U.S.? Clearly, our present policy, to the extent it is applied at all, is not working. Formal deportations number only about 160,000 a year, most of whom are criminals or terrorists. An estimated 500,000 aliens who have received deportation orders are running loose in the U.S. Many of those actually deported return to the U.S., a felony which U.S. attorneys lack time or willingness to prosecute. About 1.3 million are caught each year by ICE (Immigration and Customs Enforcement) at or near the border, and until recently either released on their own recognizance if non-Mexican, or given voluntary departure back to Mexico with no penalties.

The sanctions enacted against willful employers of illegal aliens have all but been abandoned by our federal government. A patchwork of ongoing partial amnesty programs and other loopholes legalizes some 180,000 illegal aliens a year.

A Lack of Enforcement

A 2005 Government Accountability Office (GAO) report found that ICE man-hours spent on work site enforcement fell from an already inadequate 240 in 1999 to just 90 in 2003. Other enforcement indicators such as arrests of persistent violators, employer fine notices, and work site arrests declined even more steeply. While Washington blamed changed priorities after 9/11 [the terrorist attacks against the United States on September 11, 2001], the cutbacks started almost two years before 9/11 when the economic boom of the late 1990s sparked employer complaints of labor shortages.

Washington's leniency and indifference deeply trouble more and more Americans.

Without consistent detection and tough penalties for illegal employment and illegal presence, it will remain next to impossible for the border patrol to halt the influx of millions of illegal aliens. One of the reasons for this futility is obvious. There is now no effective penalty for crossing our borders illegally. In 99 percent of the cases a Mexican illegal alien now apprehended at our border is simply recorded, fingerprinted, checked for criminal history and prior attempted entry, and then transported back across the border to Mexico. Once across, he or she is free to try again. Many do, often the same night.

Eventually, those who persist do succeed. That is why there are two to three million illegal border crossings each year, with over 500,000 new illegal aliens who settle each year. The entire system, if it were not tragic, would be almost comical. It is a very elaborate, expensive game known to the [U.S.] Border Patrol as "catch and release." Illegal aliens have no trouble calculating that the benefits of succeeding outweigh the risks of capture.

American Opinion on Illegal Immigration

Washington's leniency and indifference deeply trouble more and more Americans. A national poll commissioned by NPG [Negative Population Growth] and carried out in March 2003 by RoperASW found that more than 60 percent of Americans agree that:

- Congress should set a goal of halting *completely* the annual settlement of new illegal entrants, currently estimated at 500,000 to 600,000.

- Congress should set a goal of reducing the estimated 10 million to 15 million resident illegal immigrants to near zero.

- Congress should make penalties for illegal presence here so severe that no illegal immigrants would come here or remain here. Our legislators should enact such tough measures as mandatory fines and prison terms for anyone found to be here illegally, or attempting to enter illegally, followed by deportation and a permanent ban on return. . . .

Requiring Verification of Legal Status

We need a comprehensive federal program that would make it virtually impossible for an illegal immigrant to remain here undetected. The heart of the program would be to require government authorities or private sector officials to confirm legal status whenever anyone:

- Attempts to open a bank account, purchase bank instruments or securities, or transfer money abroad.

- Applies for a driver's or pilot's license, or any other commercial or occupational license.

- Seeks to enroll in school or college for oneself or one's children.

- Seeks medical care at a hospital. (Emergency care would be provided.)

- Applies for a marriage license, birth certificate or other vital document.

- Applies for a social security number. (Now required.)

- Applies for a job. (Already required, though verification is inadequate.)

- Attempts to buy, sell or rent real estate.

- Applies for a credit card or any other form of credit.

- Seeks to purchase, rent or register a vehicle, aircraft, firearm, explosives, or controlled hazardous materials.

There are precedents for such screening, and databases exist to make it work. A prototype is USCIS's [U.S. Citizenship and Immigration Services'] Systematic Alien Verification for Entitlements (SAVE) in use since 1987 to verify the legal status of persons seeking certain federally controlled state and local benefits. A variety of state and local agencies that need to confirm legal status have voluntarily signed on to SAVE, such as the California DMV [Department of Motor Vehicles], City of New York Human Resources Administration, the Palm Beach County Property Appraiser, and the Michigan tribal gaming commission.

It would be impossible to effectively enforce tougher penalties and more frequent screening without committed cooperation from local and state law enforcement.

Verification of legal status would, for the time being, continue to be by a telephone or online check to a central database maintained by the U.S. government. Until biometric ID documents are adopted, screening should not depend exclusively on any document presented by the applicant. (U.S. passports and some biometric state driver's licenses, for example, would be an exception.) Local law enforcement authorities should be alerted immediately if an illegal alien applicant is detected.

The Role of State and Local Governments

It would be impossible to effectively enforce tougher penalties and more frequent screening without committed cooperation from local and state law enforcement. While there are only approximately 2,000 interior enforcement immigration agents to police the entire country, there are approximately 600,000 local and state law enforcement agents. Federal law now provides for training and assistance to state and local law enforcement agencies that volunteer. State and local agencies need full authority to enforce immigration law and their participation should be mandatory.

Public opinion would be behind it. The increasingly apparent link between illegal immigration, crime and drugs has made state and local governments more receptive to a role in immigration. NPG's RoperASW poll found that 88% of respondents favored Congress requiring state and local governments to apprehend and turn over to ICE illegal immigrants they encounter. A number of states have accepted the option provided in 1996 legislation for federal training and assistance to state and local police on immigration enforcement. H.R. 4733, passed in December 2005, fully empowers state and local police to enforce immigration laws.

With such laws and procedures consistently and strictly applied, the country would no longer need to debate whether, for example, illegal aliens should be issued a driver's license, or receive favorable tuition rates at colleges. The obvious answer to both questions is that illegal aliens should not remain here at all.

There are precedents for believing that large-scale self-deportation is feasible and realistic.

The Objection to Deportation

Proponents of mass immigration and even some high government officials argue that we must simply accept the fact that nothing can be done to eliminate, or even seriously reduce, the number of resident illegal aliens. They claim it to be impossible for the government to round up and deport 10 to 15 million people. Often they put this in terms of the most unappealing and impractical option, a "mass roundup." Another common objection to proposed prison terms, fines and forfeitures is the argument that it would swamp our federal courts and prisons.

This need not be so. If the penalties and detection processes are sustained and evenly applied, there would be major changes in the illegal aliens' perceptions, leading to their extensive self-deportation over time. The near certainty of detection, apprehension, jail terms and fines would attach a prohibitively high price to violations. Federal court overload in the interim could be avoided by much broader use of "expedited deportation" (i.e., without hearings), and by continuing to treat first-time illegal entry as a misdemeanor with a penalty of a fine and not more than one-year jail time. Misdemeanors can usually be disposed of in one day by federal courts.

There are precedents for believing that large-scale self-deportation is feasible and realistic.

Examples of Tough Enforcement

The best example of tough enforcement changing behavior, of course, is the mass removals of 1954. Then, the apprehensions by INS [U.S. Immigration and Naturalization Service] of some one million illegal aliens over a few months in a determined sweep produced tens of thousands of self-deportations and suppressed illegal immigration for a decade thereafter.

In the summer of 1988, there was a great deal of unrest in Central America, and over 1,000 illegal aliens crossed the Texas border near Brownsville and Harlingen daily. At the outset, for foreign policy reasons, they were released on their own recognizance to apply for asylum. But in a policy switch, then attorney general [Edwin] Meese ordered that the intercepted aliens denied immediate asylum be held in detention or otherwise prevented from leaving south Texas. Soon the stream of illegals dropped from over 1,000 a day to almost none.

More recently, in December 2005 the flow of Brazilian and some other non-Mexican illegal aliens through Mexico dropped sharply once ICE began detaining and removing them under its "expedited deportation" authority. Full success of this policy will require adequate detention space for sizeable numbers of illegal aliens.

In a November 2003 paper the Center for Immigration Studies, a Washington research organization, took note of the government's 9/11 "Special Registration" program for visitors from Islamic countries. The Muslim nation with the most illegal aliens present was Pakistan with an estimated 26,000. Once it became clear that Homeland Security was serious about enforcing the law on Middle Easterners, Pakistani illegal aliens "self-deported" in droves to Pakistan, Canada, and Europe. The Pakistani embassy estimated that more than 15,000 of its nationals had left the country.

The mass exodus by Pakistani illegals occurred because of the likelihood of detection and without an explicit threat of jail time. With credible high prospects of detection followed by a heavy fine and/or prison for illegal presence, we are convinced that a substantial portion of the millions of illegal aliens now living here would, within months, leave the country on their own. . . .

The Importance of Halting Illegal Immigration

Our primary concern with immigration, both legal and illegal, is that it adds weightily to population growth in our crowded country. Our present population of 298 million is already far beyond the long-term carrying capacity of our resources and environment. We need to halt, and eventually reverse our population growth so that, after an interim period of population decline, we can stabilize our population at a lower, sustainable level.

If there were no other reasons to end illegal immigration, homeland security alone would be sufficient.

Besides its impact on our population size, there are a number of other compelling reasons for halting illegal immigration. First, the violation of our laws by millions of illegal aliens breeds contempt for all laws and nourishes a culture of fraud and deceit. Illegal aliens depress wages of American citizens and legal immigrants, and add to their unemployment. Their access to social services combined with their low tax payments burden our taxpayers. The claim is often made that they do jobs that Americans will not do, but there are no jobs that Americans will not do with proper work conditions and wages. Their presence invites abuse by unscrupulous employers, and results in the creation of thousands of sweatshops and a pernicious underground economy.

The annual flow of illegal aliens across our borders and the presence of many millions who live here clandestinely is an open invitation to terrorists to establish themselves in our country and attack us. If there were no other reasons to end illegal immigration, homeland security alone would be sufficient. It is outrageous that over four years after 9/11, our federal government has done so little to halt illegal immigration and secure our borders.

The Problems of Underdeveloped Countries

Principally because of the disparity between our standard of living and that of most third world countries, hundreds of millions of people are determined to come here, whether legally or illegally. Most third world people live in abject poverty, and we sympathize with their plight. World population is growing by some 77 million a year, and almost all of that growth occurs in the developing countries, the countries that send us almost all illegal immigrants. We cannot possibly allow more than a tiny fraction of those millions to come here each year without degrading our quality of life and environment.

Clearly, to believe that the problems of underdeveloped countries can be solved by emigration is delusional. Nothing can permanently and significantly improve living conditions in those countries unless they halt and eventually reverse their population growth, the root cause of their economic and environmental poverty. We should do everything in our power to help those impoverished nations that are determined to halt, and eventually to reverse, their population growth.

If that is ever to happen, it will take decades and perhaps centuries. Because of the tremendous momentum of past population growth in the third world and the resulting disproportionate numbers of young people, just slowing growth is a gargantuan task. Despite official optimism, an eventual halt to population growth in third world countries may well occur because of increased mortality rather than reduced fertility.

The US National Interest

In the meantime, we need not feel apologetic for giving top priority to our own national interest, by halting illegal immigration completely and drastically reducing legal immigration. The U.S. has a long history of generous immigration policies. Our first and primary responsibility now must be to provide for the welfare of present and future generations of Americans, many of them descendants of earlier immigrants, and alleviate environmental pressures in the U.S., such as global warming, that are threatening the whole world.

As world population continues to grow, and as that growth continues to degrade economic and environmental conditions in many third world countries, the push factors abroad will inevitably increase in force and intensity.

U.S.-bound migration verges on becoming a tidal wave of irresistible force. An irresistible force can only be stopped by an immovable object—and that can only be our own nation's unshakable resolve to stop illegal immigration and reduce to near zero the illegal population now here.

Failure to Enforce Laws Has Resulted in an Illegal Immigration Crisis

William Gheen

William Gheen is president and spokesman for Americans for Legal Immigration PAC (ALIPAC), a political action committee dedicated to fighting against illegal immigration.

Today, Americans face an unprecedented illegal immigration crisis facilitated by multibillion-dollar drug and human importing cartels as well as corporations which are inducing the invasion by aiding and abetting illegal aliens and using their influence on the executive branch and elections to paralyze existing immigration laws supported by over 80% of the American citizenry.

These events are not random and chaotic. Massive illegal immigration is the result of non-enforcement and under-enforcement of our existing immigration laws.

The Will of the American Public

Supporters of illegal aliens love to claim that our immigration system is broken. The system is not broken. Elite financial and political business interests who could care less about the death and devastation they are causing Americans have sabotaged the system. Their profits continue to rise as they send the rest of America spiraling downward on a path to anarchy and Third World quality-of-life conditions.

By using their influence to suspend our existing laws, these globalist special interests have deprived all Americans of political representation as well as their votes, their voice, and a functioning republic for which our flag stands.

When the laws of the American people—debated and voted on by their duly elected congressional representatives and signed into law by the president—go intentionally under-enforced by the executive branch, all of the principles, sovereignty, and self-governance of Americans are derailed. The will of the American public, the existing laws, the US Constitution, and the borders of our great nation are perceived as market hindrances to the global elite. We the people of America are perceived as peasants and subjects beneath the power of their influence.

The truth is that most Americans want the illegal aliens to return to the nations of which they are citizens.

The American public has spoken through our lawmakers and in numerous polls. A super majority of Americans want our existing laws enforced, those responsible for illegal immigration fined and/or imprisoned, the borders secured, and illegal aliens deported from the United States for many years or permanently. These facts remain, despite several politicized polls which attempt to manufacture consent and make you believe such views represent a minority.

The truth is that most Americans want the illegal aliens to return to the nations of which they are citizens. The rallying cry is: "Illegals Go Home!"

The Importance of Deterrence

We could easily list 101 reasons why Americans are upset about illegal immigration. Most are concerned about the 4,000+ preventable deaths of Americans by the criminal acts of illegal aliens on our soil each year. No corporate propaganda will change the fact that most Americans do not want to surrender or capitulate to the lawless masses rushing into our nation.

No poll or politicized source is needed to prove this point because the decision is based upon our nation's successful history and basic common sense. The answer is based on something that every judge, lawmaker, and even street thug knows. The penalties must outweigh the benefits if you want to deter any action.

It is common sense and common practice in America that for any law to be a deterrent, two important factors are in play. First, the laws must be enforced, and second, the penalties for any crime must exceed the benefits to those breaking the law.

It is truly amazing that we find ourselves as a nation having to explain these basic foundations of law to corporations and politicians in the year 2007 despite their existence since the dawn of civilization! Can you imagine what would happen in America if the penalty for robbing a bank was that you had to return half of the money you stole if, and only if, you were apprehended for the crime? What if the penalty for car theft was paying a $2,000 fine if you were caught with the stolen vehicle?

The answers are clear. Within a month, you would not have a bank open in America and you would not be able to keep a car worth more than $2,000 in your driveway for more than a week. How many millions of people would quickly take up the careers of bank robber and car thief once the rewards for the crime were higher than the penalty?

If American businesses and homes left their windows and doors unlocked each night and robbers were merely removed by police when detected—only to try again the next night— what do you think would happen? If big, global businesses practiced the same non-enforcement of security similar to the lack of border security and lack of immigration enforcement they have facilitated for Americans, they would be out of business in a matter of days or weeks. If they left their doors unlocked at night and just pushed people back to the street,

America would quickly descend into such chaos and anarchy that we would be unable to sustain a population of 300 million. Our population would take a hit similar to the impact of the Black Plague on Europe, and we would quickly enter a new dark age.

Attrition Through Enforcement

Since illegal aliens can never afford to compensate Americans for what they have taken, they must go. We do not need to go door to door looking for illegals to deport in America. Attrition through enforcement works. Illegal aliens are leaving the states of Georgia and Pennsylvania in droves, not because they are enforcing the laws but because they have simply announced they plan to start!

Unfortunately, the current state of affairs in America has illegals flooding in by the millions each year and many law-abiding Americans fleeing the states of California and Texas and many towns and cities in search of more safety and security. Many Americans are on the run and finding few places left to run to.

Attrition through enforcement will work.

The illegal aliens are sending a clear message on the streets of Los Angeles and other major urban centers. They are saying: "This is our land. White, black, and legal Hispanics get out!"

This is great news for the housing and real estate markets, Wal-Mart, and McDonald's. They are growing the economy using rapid population growth. This is great news for big corporations and bad news for Americans.

Attrition through enforcement will work. In fact, if President George [W.] Bush were to announce on national television that America would begin securing our borders and enforcing our existing laws in one month, so many illegal aliens would leave America that Mexico would have to set up refuge stations!

Another important reason that the illegal aliens must leave for the long term is that they'll return to their home communities with a message for their neighbors that their ill-gotten gains did not pay off in America. This is the only thing that will stop, or slow, the flow. Deporting illegal aliens and sending them packing is the only real way we can put a stop to this crisis.

Legislation That Does Not Work

The politicians in [Washington,] D.C., are very aware that Americans want the illegal aliens to go. That is why their latest Scamnesty legislation includes a "touchback" provision. Under these laws, the illegal aliens can hop across the Mexican or Canadian borders where special "Ellis Island" stations are set up for them to pay a fine, receive new documentation and be back in the US within days or hours.

The lunatics advocating this plan are counting on Americans to be so stupid and so gullible that they can say, "Look, the illegals left and walked back in legally. Problem solved!" They are eager to pretend to accommodate the American desires for the illegals to leave while quickly returning their slave labor force to our nation.

They know that Americans want illegals to leave and get behind a long line of legal immigrants waiting to enter the US, including millions of people who have been waiting 5–10 years. These politicians and the illegal aliens need to be shown the way to the back of the line. The back of the line is back in the country in which they are citizens, 5–10 years down the road behind all of the talented and law-abiding people who respect our laws.

If these traitorous corporations and politicians succeed in setting up these Ellis Island stations for "Operation Touchback," the revered symbol of Ellis Island will take on a new meaning that Americans see with contempt and resentment. Ellis Island will become a name associated with the horrendous betrayal of free Americans and the deathblow to the American Republic. This is a symbol of America's surrender and the subjugation of all her people.

If we allow the politicians in D.C. to sign off on the many Guest Worker, Temporary Worker, Path to Citizenship, Amnesty, Scamnesty bills written by the US Chamber of Commerce, then no wall with an army on top of it will stop the next 20 million from crashing down on our country. We will have signaled that America is weak and will capitulate and accommodate. Already, the word is out in Central and South America that they can come and stay. Each time President Bush has opened his mouth about such programs, the US Border Patrol reports massive spikes in illegal crossings.

The Need for a Crackdown

Since there is literally no end to the stream of illegals who want to be in America, this will be the end of America as we have known it and as history has praised it.

In the past, when America has cracked down on illegal immigration and the American people have signaled they want the immigration brakes applied, the policies have worked. New laws written near the turn of the 20th century greatly reduced the amount of immigration into America. When Presidents Franklin Roosevelt and Dwight Eisenhower launched large deportation campaigns in the 1930s and 1950s, illegal immigration slowed to minuscule levels as a result.

Whether you agree or disagree with the decisions of the past, these policies were part of the successful formula that have led America to become the most opulent and successful civilization in human history.

While some argue that these enforcement measures were racist and that some American citizens of different races were improperly deported at the time, we now have the technology and methodology in place to assure that American citizens and legal immigrants are not improperly affected by our immigration enforcement efforts.

The difference in 2007 is that the globalist corporations that have hijacked the American government want to stop the American citizenry from applying the brakes this time. They have taken away our ability to determine who can enter our nation and our ability to stop armed and unarmed invasions as granted by the US Constitution.

To take away the self-governance of Americans is to kill the very thing that has made us such a great and successful nation.

In a time of crisis like this, we must stand firm on the principles that have made America an attractive and great nation. We must stand firm on the rule of law. The law must be applied equally to big corporations and illegal aliens alike lest we all become slaves subject to the plans of masters instead of a free and empowered citizenry.

The illegals must go.

Illegal aliens and corporations must endure penalties for their illegal, deadly, and destructive actions that exceed the benefits they gain from their illegal activities.

The hour is late and it is time for Americans to stand up and say with one voice . . .

No Amnesty! No Guest Worker! Secure our borders and enforce the existing laws! Restore the American Republic!

The illegals must go.

Illegals go home!

Immigration, Legal and Illegal, Improves the Lives of Americans

Daniel Griswold

Daniel Griswold is director of the Center for Trade Policy Studies at the Cato Institute and the author of Mad About Trade: Why Main Street America Should Embrace Globalization.

Congress and President [Barack] Obama may tackle the controversial issue of immigration reform as soon as the fall of 2009. If past congressional debates are any guide, one point of contention will be the impact of reform on the American underclass.

The Argument Against Immigration

In 2006, and again in 2007, the U.S. Senate debated "comprehensive immigration reform" designed to curb illegal immigration by ramping up enforcement while providing expanded opportunities for legal immigration. Both bills would have legalized several million immigrants currently in the United States illegally and created a temporary visa program to allow more low-skilled workers to enter the country legally in future years.

One argument raised against expanded legal immigration has been that allowing more low-skilled, foreign-born workers to enter the United States will swell the ranks of the underclass. The critics warn that by "importing poverty," immigration reform would bring in its wake rising rates of poverty, higher government welfare expenditures, and a rise in crime. The argument resonates with many Americans concerned about the expanding size of government and a perceived breakdown in social order.

As plausible as the argument sounds, it is not supported by the social and economic trends of the past 15 years. Even though the number of legal and illegal immigrants in the United States has risen strongly since the early 1990s, the size of the economic underclass has not. In fact, by several measures the number of Americans living on the bottom rungs of the economic ladder has been in a long-term decline, even as the number of immigrants continues to climb. Other indicators associated with the underclass, such as the crime rate, have also shown improvement. The inflow of low-skilled immigrants may even be playing a positive role in pushing native-born Americans up the skill and income ladder.

The Size and Composition of the Underclass

"Underclass" is not a precise term, but it is generally understood to mean those who live below or near the poverty line and who lack the education or jobs skills to join the middle class. If we define the underclass to be the number of people in the United States living below the poverty line, in households earning less than $25,000 a year or without a high school diploma, and then examine the changing size and composition of each of those categories by either race or citizenship status, a consistent pattern emerges.

Even though the number of legal and illegal immigrants in the United States has risen strongly since the early 1990s, the size of the economic underclass has not.

By all three measures, the size of the underclass has been shrinking since the early 1990s—during a period of large-scale legal and illegal immigration. The composition of the underclass has also been changing, with the number of immigrants and Hispanics growing, while the number of native-born and non-Hispanics has declined at an even more rapid rate.

Families and Individuals Below the Poverty Level

If we define the underclass as families living below the official poverty level, the recent trend has been downward. Between 1995 and 2004, the number of family households living below the poverty level fell by half a million, from 8.1 million to 7.6 million. The number of immigrant households in poverty did indeed rise—by 194,000—but that increase was more than offset by a drop of 675,000 in native-born households living in poverty. In other words, for every poor immigrant family we "imported" during that time, more than three native-born families were "exported" from poverty.

Poverty figures by race span a longer period, 1993 through 2007, but they tell the same story. The total number of family households living in poverty fell by 770,000 during that period, from 8.4 million to 7.6 million. The number of Hispanic families living in poverty increased by 420,000—providing evidence of a growing Hispanic/immigrant underclass—but over those same years, the number of non-Hispanic families in poverty dropped by 1.1 million, including a decline of 408,000 in the number of poor black families.

The trend is no different when we look at individuals in poverty. From 1993 through 2007, the number of individuals in our society subsisting below the poverty line declined by 2 million, from 39.3 million to 37.3 million. A 1.8 million increase in the number of Hispanics living in poverty was swamped by a 3.8 million decline in non-Hispanics, including a 1.6 million decline in black poverty. Similarly, a 1 million increase in immigrants living in poverty was more than matched by a 3 million drop in native-born Americans under the poverty line. Measured by the official poverty numbers, the American underclass has been shrinking as it has become composed of more immigrants and more Hispanics.

Households with Income Less than $25,000

Measuring the underclass by household income reveals the same underlying trend. The number of households earning less than $25,000 in a given year dropped by 5.6 million from 1995 to 2004, according to the most recent numbers that disaggregate the underclass by citizenship status. Almost all the drop was accounted for by a decline in nonimmigrant households earning less than $25,000, which dropped from 20.6 million in 1995 to 15.0 million in 2004. (All incomes were measured in inflation-adjusted dollars.) The number of immigrant families under that income threshold also dropped, but only by 80,000. As a result, the immigrant share of the underclass grew from 15 percent to 20 percent, even as the size of the underclass was shrinking.

The same picture emerges when we examine the number of low-income households by race and ethnicity. From 1994 through 2007, the number of households in America getting by on less than $25,000 fell by almost 10 million (with incomes measured across the years in real dollars). The share of total households living under that threshold dropped from 40 percent to 25 percent. Again, the entire decline was accounted for by non-Hispanic households, including a drop of 900,000 in black households, while the number of Hispanic households surviving on less than $25,000 was virtually unchanged.

Although the underclass became increasingly more Hispanic during the period, the share of all households living on less than $25,000 fell for every ethnic group. In fact, the steepest decline in percentage terms was among Hispanic households, with the share of households living below $25,000 dropping from 53 percent to 31 percent.

Householders and Individuals Without a High School Diploma

A third way of measuring the underclass is by householders or individuals without a high school diploma. In America today, a worker or head of household without a high school education is almost invariably confined to lower-productivity, and thus, lower-wage occupations, with limited prospects for advancement.

As with the poverty and income measures, here, too, the story is basically positive. Between 1993 and 2006, the number of households headed by someone 18 and older without a high school diploma dropped by 3.7 million, from 19.9 million to 16.2 million. The number of such "low-skilled households" headed by a Hispanic did indeed increase by 1.8 million during that period, undoubtedly driven in significant part by large inflows of low-skilled immigrants from Mexico and Central America. The rest of the story, however, is that during those same years, the number of non-Hispanic households headed by a high school dropout fell by a hefty 5.5 million. That means that for every net addition of one Hispanic-headed, low-skilled household to the ranks of the underclass, the number of such non-Hispanic households dropped by three. Meanwhile, the share of total U.S. households headed by a high school dropout declined steadily, from one in five to one in seven.

The number of individuals 25 years and older without a high school diploma has also been in steady decline. From 1993 through 2006, the number of adults who were high school dropouts declined from 32.1 million to 27.9 million, a fall of 4.2 million. The number of adult Hispanics in the United States without a high school education swelled by 3.9 million, much of that growth driven by the influx of low-skilled illegal immigrants. But during that same period, the number of non-Hispanic adults toiling in life without a high school diploma plunged by 8.1 million, including a drop of 1 million in the number of adult black dropouts. For every additional Hispanic dropout added to the pool, the number of non-Hispanic dropouts fell by two. The share of adults without a diploma dropped in every racial and ethnic group, although the decline was less rapid among Hispanics.

The arrival of low-skilled, foreign-born workers in the labor force increases the incentives for younger native-born Americans to stay in school.

Educational attainment by citizenship status covers a slightly different period but also confirms the trend. From 1995 to 2004, the number of adults without a high school diploma declined by 2.9 million. An increase of 2.4 million in the number of immigrant dropouts was overwhelmed by a decline of 5.3 million in native-born dropouts. As that measure of the underclass shrank, the share represented by immigrants grew from 22 percent to 32 percent. By this and the other measures above, "the underclass" in our society has been shrinking as its face has become more Hispanic and foreign-born.

Immigrants Move In, Americans Move Up

Multiple causes lie behind the shrinking of the underclass in the past 15 years. The single biggest factor is probably economic growth. Despite the current recession, the U.S. economy enjoyed healthy growth during most of the period, lifting median household incomes and real compensation earned by U.S. workers, which ushered millions of families into the middle class and beyond. Welfare reform in the 1990s and rising levels of education may also be contributing factors.

Another factor may be immigration itself. The arrival of low-skilled, foreign-born workers in the labor force increases the incentives for younger native-born Americans to stay in school and for older workers to upgrade their skills. Because they compete directly with the lowest-skilled Americans, low-skilled immigrants do exert mild downward pressure on the wages of the lowest-paid American workers. But the addition of low-skilled immigrants also expands the size of the overall economy, creating openings in higher-paid occupations such as managers, skilled craftsmen, and accountants. The result is a greater financial reward for finishing high school and for acquiring additional job skills. Immigration of low-skilled workers motivates Americans, who might otherwise languish in the underclass, to acquire the education and skills necessary so they are not competing directly with foreign-born workers.

The shrinking of the native-born underclass contradicts the argument that low-skilled immigration is particularly harmful to African Americans, who are disproportionately represented in the underclass. By each of the three measures above—poverty, income, and educational attainment—the number of black American households and individuals in the underclass has been declining. Native-born blacks have been moving up along with other native-born Americans as immigrants have been moving in.

A Win-Win Dynamic

That same win-win dynamic may have been at work a century ago during the "great migration" of immigrants from eastern and southern Europe. Most of those immigrants were lower-skilled compared with Americans, and their influx also exerted downward pressure on the wages of lower-skilled Americans. It was probably not a coincidence that during that same period the number of Americans staying in school to earn a high school diploma increased dramatically in what is called "the high school movement." From 1910 to 1940, the share of American 18-year-olds graduating from high school rose from less than 10 percent to 50 percent in a generation. Today's immigrants are arguably contributing to the same positive dynamic.

America's experience with immigration contradicts the simplistic argument that the arrival of a certain number of low-skilled immigrants increases the underclass by that very same amount. That approach ignores the dynamic and positive effects of immigration on native-born American workers. The common calculation that every low-skilled immigrant simply adds to the underclass betrays a static and inaccurate view of American society.

One striking fact about low-skilled immigrants in America, both legal and illegal, is their propensity to work.

A Less Dysfunctional Underclass

Another contribution of immigration has been that it has changed the character of the American underclass for the better. Years of low-skilled immigration have created an underclass that is not only smaller than it was 15 years ago, but also more functional. Members of today's more immigrant and Hispanic underclass are more likely to work and less likely to live in poverty or commit crimes than members of the more native-born underclass of past decades.

One striking fact about low-skilled immigrants in America, both legal and illegal, is their propensity to work. In 2008, the labor force participation rate of foreign-born Hispanics was 70.7 percent—compared to an overall rate of 65.6 percent for native-born Americans. Immigrants 25 years of age or older, without a high school diploma, were half again more likely to be participating in the labor force than native-born dropouts (61.1 percent vs. 38.4 percent). According to estimates by the Pew Hispanic Center, male illegal immigrants, ages 18–64, had a labor force participation rate in 2004 of an incredible 92 percent. Illegal immigrants are typically poor, but they are almost all working poor.

Immigrants and Crime

Nowhere is the contrast between the immigrant and native-born underclass more striking than in their propensity to commit crimes. Across all ethnicities and educational levels, immigrants are less prone to commit crimes and land in prison than their native-born counterparts.

The reasons behind this phenomenon are several. Legal immigrants can be screened for criminal records, reducing the odds that they will engage in criminal behavior once in the United States. Illegal immigrants have the incentive to avoid committing crimes to minimize their chances of being caught and deported. Legal or illegal, immigrants come to America to realize the opportunities of working in a more free-market, open, and prosperous economy; committing a crime puts that opportunity in jeopardy.

Strong empirical evidence points to the fact that immigrants are less likely to commit crimes than native-born Americans. In testimony before Congress in 2007, Anne Morrison Piehl, a professor of criminal justice at Rutgers University, addressed the question of "The Connection Between Immigration and Crime." Using census data from 1980, 1990, and 2000, she told the House Judiciary Committee that "immigrants have much lower institutionalization rates than the native born—on the order of one-fifth the rate of natives. More-recently-arrived immigrants had the lowest relative institutionalization rates, and the gap with natives increased from 1980 to 2000." Piehl found no evidence that the immigrant crime rate was lower because of the deportation of illegal immigrants who might otherwise be held behind bars in the United States.

The National Crime Rate

Crime rates are even lower than average among the poorly educated and Hispanic immigrants that arouse the most concern from skeptics of immigration reform. Rubén [G.] Rumbaut of the University of California at Irvine, after examining the 2000 census data, found that incarceration rates among both legal and illegal immigrants from Mexico, El Salvador, and Guatemala were all less than half the rate of U.S.-born whites. Immigrants without a high school diploma had an incarceration rate that was one-fourth that of native-born high school graduates, and one-seventh that of native-born dropouts.

> *Illegal immigrants who break U.S. immigration laws to enter the United States appear much more likely than native-born Americans to respect our domestic criminal code once they are inside.*

The reluctance of low-skilled immigrants to commit crimes helps to explain the lack of any noticeable connection between rising levels of illegal immigration and the overall national crime rate. As Professor Rumbaut explained in a recent essay:

> Since the early 1990s, over the same time period as legal and especially illegal immigration was reaching and surpassing historic highs, crime rates have *declined*, both nationally and most notably in cities and regions of high immigrant concentrations (including cities with large numbers of undocumented immigrants, such as Los Angeles, and border cities like San Diego and El Paso, as well as New York, Chicago, and Miami).

Ironically, illegal immigrants who break U.S. immigration laws to enter the United States appear much more likely than native-born Americans to respect our domestic criminal code once they are inside the country. Once here, low-skilled immigrants, as a rule, get down to the business of earning money, sending home remittances, and staying out of trouble. The wider benefit to our society is that, in comparison to 15 years ago, a member of today's underclass, standing on a street corner, is more likely to be waiting for a job than a drug deal.

Contrary to popular notions, low-skilled immigration has not contributed to a swelling of the underclass, or any increase at all, nor has it contributed to a rise in crime or other antisocial behaviors. In fact, it would be more plausible to argue that low-skilled immigration has actually accelerated the upward mobility of Americans on the lower end of the socioeconomic ladder. At the same time, the influx of low-skilled immigrants has helped to transform the American underclass into a demographic group that is still poor—but more inclined to work and less prone to crime.

The Need to Expand Legal Immigration

Members of Congress should not reject market-oriented immigration reform because of misguided fears about "importing poverty." Based on recent experience, a policy that allows more low-skilled workers to enter the United States legally would not necessarily expand the number of people living in poverty or the number of low-skilled households demanding government services. It would not impose significant costs on American society in the form of welfare spending or crime abatement.

As Cato [Institute] research has shown elsewhere, strong, positive arguments remain for pursuing a policy of expanding legal immigration for low-skilled workers. Comprehensive immigration reform that included a robust temporary worker program would boost economic output and create new middle-class job opportunities for native-born Americans. It would reduce the inflow of illegal workers across the border, allowing enforcement resources to be redeployed more effectively to interdict terrorists and real criminals. It would restore the rule of law to U.S. immigration policy, while reducing calls for enforcement measures such as a national ID card or a centralized employment verification system, which compromise the freedom and civil liberties of American citizens.

Along with those major benefits, immigration reform would enhance the incentives for native-born Americans up and down the income ladder to acquire the education and skills they need to prosper in a dynamic economy.

Illegal Immigration Is Not a Bigger Problem than Legal Immigration

Ramesh Ponnuru

Ramesh Ponnuru is a senior editor for National Review, *a magazine of conservative politics.*

Illegal immigration is not a big problem in America. Okay, let me amend that before pots and pans and worse things come flying at me. America has some serious immigration problems, but they are not distinctively problems of illegal immigration. If we focus narrowly on illegal immigration, we are likely to come up with counterproductive solutions.

Complaints About Illegal Immigration

Almost all of the things that cause people to complain about illegal immigration are true of much legal immigration as well. If your worry is that illegal immigrants tend to raise government spending, for example, then you ought to be worried about legal immigrants, too. Half of legal immigrants have not gone past high school. Like illegal immigrants, they cost federal and state governments billions of dollars each year.

Or perhaps you're concerned that illegal immigrants hurt low-income workers by driving low-end wages down. If so, you should be almost as concerned about legal immigration. Illegal immigrants tend to be paid less than legal immigrants, but the difference is small and largely reflects the fact that on average illegal immigrants have slightly less education than legal immigrants.

Maybe you're afraid that the United States is importing social problems through illegal immigration. Without illegal immigration, we would have fewer poor people and fewer people without health insurance. There would be less strain on our health care system and less likelihood that your taxes will go up in the future to take care of these problems. The difference with legal immigration, especially the unskilled kind, is one of degree.

Almost all of the things that cause people to complain about illegal immigration are true of much legal immigration as well.

If what most disturbs you is the possibility that illegal immigrants will not assimilate to our society, again, you have to have qualms about legal immigration. An immigrant who lacks legal status will probably not assimilate as easily as someone who has it, since he will not participate as fully in American life. But the sheer number of immigrants, legal and illegal, is probably a more important determinant of assimilation (especially when so many of them come from the same place). The immigrant population grows by about 1 million people annually. Half are legal, half illegal.

And if you're concerned about immigrant voting patterns, as many Republicans are, at least in private, then you ought to object much more to legal than to illegal immigration. Illegal immigrants can't vote for tax-raising, big-government politicians (although they can slightly increase the number of Democratic legislators through their effect on apportionment and districting).

The national security argument for cracking down on illegal immigration is that "we need to know who's here." But our immigration bureaucracy is not extraordinarily competent or well supported. It does not do a great job of processing the existing flow of legal immigrants through the system. If that legal flow stays at its current volume, there is a limit to how helpful that bureaucracy can be to law enforcement.

In practice, legal and illegal immigration are pretty closely linked. Legal and illegal immigrants come from the same places, both categories being dominated by Mexicans. They live in many of the same neighborhoods, even the same households, and often work for the same employers. James Edwards of the Hudson Institute points out that the numbers for both categories have risen in tandem. People sometimes make it sound as though increases in legal immigration will meet businesses' needs and thus drive down their demand for illegal-immigrant labor. But any such effect is hard to see in the numbers.

Respect for the Law

The best argument for considering illegal immigration a distinctive problem is that it undermines respect for the law. But this harm is pretty abstract. It drives popular anxiety about illegal immigration only in the sense that illegal immigration is a symbol of a larger immigration policy that cannot command respect. It points to our political elites' failure to take seriously the responsibility to determine how many people, and which people, we will let in—and that is something that people are capable of getting plenty mad about.

So why do so many people say that they are against illegal immigration but for legal immigration? In part, it's because the distinction creates a handy rhetorical club for the person who makes it. It puts the other side in the position of defending, or seeming to defend, illegality. But I suspect that it's mostly because making the distinction is a way to look reasonable, moderate, and non-racist. "I have no problem with immigrants. My grandparents were immigrants! I just have a problem with the ones who come here illegally." You're objecting to a type of behavior, not a type of person.

And since illegal immigrants have done something bad—broken the law—it is more acceptable to think ill of them than of legal immigrants. Thus it is easy to blame them for the failures of our immigration policy.

There are better ways to be humanitarian. Illegal immigrants come here for the same reasons legal immigrants do: chiefly, to make a better life for themselves and their families. That is not an ignoble ambition; it is one that deserves sympathy and even admiration. The illegal immigrant's law-breaking is wrong, but understandable, and not gravely wrong.

An Overfocus on Illegal Immigration

My point here is not to make a case for an immigration policy but to offer some notes on how to think (and how not to think) about immigration. But I do have some views on what that policy should be. I think that America would assimilate its migrants better, more easily, and faster if the total number of immigrants each year—legal and illegal—were brought down. I think that more assimilation would bring a range of benefits to native-born Americans, to those immigrants we let in, and to future immigrants. I don't think that it is necessary to be angry at immigrants, legal or illegal, to believe these things.

To come up with a rational immigration policy, we have to be able to hold two thoughts simultaneously. Immigrants, including illegal immigrants, are human beings with rights, dignity, and legitimate interests. And there is no reason to be apologetic about pursuing our national interest. If we think (as I do) that reducing immigration would be good for the country and even, in the long run, for immigrants themselves, we should not feel that we are anti-immigrant. We should protest, in fact, if others say that we are.

If, instead, we continue to obsess about illegal immigration to the exclusion of larger concerns, we are apt to make mistakes. That obsession has distorted the debate over President [George W.] Bush's [2006] immigration proposals, causing both opponents and supporters to focus on the wrong things.

Objections have centered on the "amnesty" that critics say he would give to illegal immigrants already here. But it's the invitation to new "temporary guest workers," not the alleged amnesty to previous migrants, that is the truly momentous feature of Bush's plan. We have a de facto amnesty already, since we're not enforcing immigration laws. We don't have a temporary-worker program.

If . . . we continue to obsess about illegal immigration to the exclusion of larger concerns, we are apt to make mistakes.

Some supporters of the president's plan speculate that it could bring total immigration levels down. The argument is that illegal immigrants never leave the U.S. because they are afraid they would have trouble coming back. Let them come and go legally, and fewer of them would settle here. I'm skeptical. But whether Bush's plan has this effect is a more important question than the endlessly disputed question of whether the plan's treatment of illegal immigrants in this country amounts to an amnesty.

The Attrition Strategy

The supporters, meanwhile, use an exaggerated horror of illegal immigration to recruit allies. The presence of millions of illegal immigrants in this country is intolerable, they say. But if deporting all of them is off the table, the only solution left is something like what the president proposes. Creating a legal channel for illegal immigrants to stay here and work—call it an amnesty if you want—is the only way to solve the problem.

As it happens, there is an alternative to deportation and amnesty. Mark Krikorian, the head of the Center for Immigration Studies, argues for an "attrition strategy." Every year, something like 700–800,000 illegal immigrants come here, 50,000 are deported, 150,000 leave, and 25,000 die. (I owe these rough estimates to Krikorian's colleague Steven [A.] Camarota.) Stepped-up enforcement of immigration laws, especially at workplaces that tend to use illegal labor, will decrease the first number and increase the second and third. Over time, such tactics could cause the illegal population to shrink.

One of the strengths of Krikorian's strategy, to my mind, is that it does not attempt to bring about an instant solution to a problem that has been decades in the making. It accepts that millions of illegal immigrants will continue to live here while trying to foster improved conditions. But the more intolerable we regard the presence of illegal immigrants, the more we will look on this strength as a weakness—and the more we will be tempted by a quick fix. Define the problem the wrong way, and you'll get the wrong solution.

Illegal Immigration from Mexico Will Cease to Be a Problem Soon

Robert M. Dunn Jr.

Robert M. Dunn Jr. was a professor of economics at George Washington University prior to his death in 2010.

As the debate over illegal immigration from Mexico rages in Washington and across the country, and as the [George W. Bush] administration's reform bill hangs by a thread [in 2007], few Americans are aware that this problem is on track to decline, and will eventually become a vague memory.

The Fertility Rate in Mexico

There has been a stunning decline in the fertility rate in Mexico, which means that, in a few years, there will not be nearly as many teenagers in Mexico looking for work in the United States or anywhere else. If this trend in the fertility rate continues, Mexico will resemble Japan and Italy—rapidly aging populations with too few young workers to support the economy.

According to the World Bank's 2007 annual development indicators, in 1990 Mexico had a total lifetime fertility rate of 3.3 children per female, but by 2005, that number had fallen by 36 percent to 2.1, which is the "break even" point for population stability in developed nations. The large number of women currently in their reproductive years means that there are still quite a few babies, but as this group ages, the number of infants will decline sharply. If this trend toward fewer children continues, there being no apparent reason for it to cease, the number of young people in the Mexican population will

Robert M. Dunn Jr., "Mexican Immigration Will Solve Itself," *American*, June 29, 2007. Copyright © 2007 by The American.

decline significantly just when the number of elderly is rising. As labor markets in Mexico tighten and wage rates rise, far fewer Mexican youngsters will be interested in coming to the United States. Since our baby boomers will be retiring at the same time, we could face a severe labor shortage.

A Demographic Transition

There have been significant declines in fertility rates across Latin America, but Mexico's has been unusually sharp. In El Salvador, another source of U.S. immigrants, the rate declined from 3.7 in 1990 to 2.5 by 2005. Guatemala is now at 4.3, but that is far lower than it was in 1990. Jamaica, another source of U.S. immigrants, has fallen from 2.9 to 2.4 over the same period. Chile and Costa Rica, at 2.0, are actually slightly below a replacement rate. Trinidad and Tobago, at 1.6, is well below ZPG [zero population growth]. For all of Latin America and the Caribbean, a rate of 3.2 in 1990 fell to 2.4 in 2005, a decline of 25 percent. This means less pressure on the United States from illegal immigrants from the entire area, not just from Mexico. A powerful demographic transition is well under way, and soon many of these countries may be worried about there being too few babies rather than too many. We may miss this labor, and wonder how we will replace it.

We have only a temporary problem with illegal immigration from Mexico.

What has changed? Better education and improved job opportunities for women mean that it has become quite expensive for them to leave the labor force to have more children. The improved availability of birth control technology and liberalization of abortion rules in some countries mean that it is easier for women to avoid that outcome.

Another reason for the particularly sharp decline in Mexico is the cultural influence of the United States. Some politicians fear that we are being "Mexicanized." In fact the opposite may be under way. NAFTA [North American Free Trade Agreement], our mass media, the more widespread use of English, and the large number of people going back and forth (legally or otherwise) mean that Mexicans are increasingly influenced by our culture, and that implies fewer babies. The United States also has a fertility rate of 2.1, but that is the same as it was in 1990. Mexico is becoming more similar to the United States, which must frustrate their nationalists.

The main point for the United States is that we have only a temporary problem with illegal immigration from Mexico. For another decade or a bit more we must attempt to limit such entry, but then the problem will fade like the smile on the Cheshire Cat. [Broadcast journalist] Lou Dobbs, Rep. [Tom] Tancredo and their nationalistic friends can calm down and relax.

CHAPTER 2

Does Illegal Immigration Harm US Citizens?

Overview: The Costs and Gains of Illegal Immigrants

Gordon H. Hanson

Gordon H. Hanson is the director of the Center on Pacific Economies and professor of economics at the University of California, San Diego.

Are the gains that illegal immigration brings in terms of labor market flexibility offset by other economic costs? Critics of illegal immigration argue that an influx of illegal immigrants brings high economic costs by lowering domestic wages and raising expenditures on public services such as health care and education. If those costs are sufficiently high, the economic case for restricting illegal immigration would be strengthened.

The Impact of Immigration on Income

Overall, immigration increases the incomes of U.S. residents by allowing the economy to utilize domestic resources more efficiently. But because immigrants of different types—illegal, legal temporary, and legal permanent—have varying skill levels, income-earning ability, family size, and rights to use public services, changes in their respective inflows have different economic impacts. Immigration also affects U.S. incomes through its impact on tax revenue and public expenditure. Immigrants with lower incomes and larger families tend to be a bigger drain on public spending. Immigrants pay income, payroll, sales, property, and other taxes, with lower-skilled immigrants making smaller contributions. Immigrants use public services by sending their kids to public schools, demanding fire and police protection, driving on roads and highways, and receiving public assistance, with families that have larger numbers of children absorbing more expenditure. Adding the pretax income gains from immigration to immigrants' net tax contributions—their tax payments less the value of government services they use—allows for a rough estimate of the net impact of immigration on the U.S. economy.

Immigration generates extra income for the U.S. economy, even as it pushes down wages for some workers. By increasing the supply of labor, immigration raises the productivity of resources that are complementary to labor. More workers allow U.S. capital, land, and natural resources to be exploited more efficiently. Increasing the supply of labor to perishable fruits and vegetables, for instance, means that each acre of land under cultivation generates more output. Similarly, an expansion in the number of manufacturing workers allows the existing industrial base to produce more goods. The gain in productivity yields extra income for U.S. businesses, which is termed the immigration surplus. The annual immigration surplus in the United States appears to be small, equal to about 0.2 percent of GDP [gross domestic product] in 2004.

These benefits, however, are not shared equally. Labor inflows from abroad redistribute income away from workers who compete with immigrants in the labor market. [Economist] George Borjas estimates that over the period 1980 to 2000 immigration contributed to a decrease in average U.S. wages of 3 percent. This estimate accounts for the total change in the U.S. labor force due to immigration, including both legal and illegal sources. Since immigration is concentrated among the low-skilled, low-skilled natives are the workers most likely to be hurt. Over the 1980 to 2000 period, wages of native workers without a high school degree fell by 9 percent as a result of immigration. On the other hand, lower wages for low-skilled labor mean lower prices for labor-intensive goods and services, especially those whose prices are set in local markets rather than through competition in global markets. Patricia Cortes finds that in the 1980s and 1990s U.S. cities with larger inflows of low-skilled immigrants experienced larger reductions in prices for housekeeping, gardening, child care, dry cleaning, and other labor-intensive, locally traded services. Lower prices for goods and services raise the real incomes of U.S. households, with most of these gains going to those in regions with large immigrant populations.

The Fiscal Consequences of Immigration

Immigration, by admitting large numbers of low-skilled individuals, may exacerbate inefficiencies associated with the country's system of public finance. If immigrants pay more in taxes than they receive in government benefits, then immigration generates a net fiscal transfer to native taxpayers. The total impact of immigration on U.S. residents—the sum of the immigration surplus (the pretax income gain) and the net fiscal transfer from immigrants—would be unambiguously positive. This appears to be the case for immigrants with high skill levels, suggesting that employment-based permanent immigrants and highly skilled temporary immigrants have a positive net impact on the U.S. economy. They generate a positive immigration surplus (by raising U.S. productivity) and make a positive net tax contribution (by adding to U.S. government coffers).

Immigration generates extra income for the U.S. economy, even as it pushes down wages for some workers.

On the other hand, if immigrants pay less in taxes than they receive in government benefits, then immigration generates a net fiscal burden on native taxpayers—native households would be making an income transfer to immigrant households. Paying for this fiscal transfer would require tax increases on natives, reductions in government benefits to natives, or increased borrowing from future generations (by issuing government debt). If immigrants are a net fiscal drain, the total impact of immigration on the United States would be positive only if the immigration surplus exceeded the fiscal transfer made to immigrants. For low-skilled immigration, whether legal or illegal, this does not appear to be the case.

Two Fiscal Case Studies

Calculating the fiscal consequences of immigration, while straightforward conceptually, is difficult in practice. To estimate correctly, one needs to know many details about the income, spending, and employment behavior of the entire population of immigrants. As a result, there are few comprehensive national level analyses of the fiscal impact of immigration. The National Research Council (NRC) has conducted detailed fiscal case studies on immigration in New Jersey and California, which have relatively large immigrant populations. In 2000, a few years after the study was conducted, the share of the foreign-born adult population was 34 percent in California and 24 percent in New Jersey, compared with 15 percent in the nation as a whole. The two states have immigrant populations with quite different skill profiles and patterns of welfare usage. In 2000, the share of immigrant households headed by someone with less than a high school education was 34 percent in California and 29 percent in the nation as a whole, but only 23 percent in New Jersey. Similarly, the share of immigrant households receiving cash benefits from welfare programs was 13 percent in California and 10 percent in the nation as a whole, but only 8 percent in New Jersey. These differences in welfare uptake are due in part to immigrants in California being less skilled and in part to California offering more generous benefits.

Based on federal, state, and local government expenditures and tax receipts, the NRC estimated that the short-run fiscal impact of immigration was negative in both New Jersey and California. In New Jersey, using data for 1989–1990, immigrant households received an average net fiscal transfer from natives of $1,500, or 3 percent of average state immigrant household income. Spread among the more numerous state native population, this amounted to an average net fiscal burden of $230 per native household, or 0.4 percent of average state native household income. In California, using data for 1994–95, immigrant households received an average net fiscal transfer of $3,500, or 9 percent of average immigrant household income, which resulted in an average fiscal burden on native households of $1,200, or 2 percent of average native household income. The impact of immigration on California is more negative because immigrant households in the state (a) are more numerous relative to the native population, (b) have more children, causing them to make greater use of public education, and (c) earn lower incomes, leading them to have lower tax payments and greater use of public assistance.

Calculating the fiscal consequences of immigration, while straightforward conceptually, is difficult in practice.

For the nation as a whole, the NRC estimated that in 1996 immigration imposed a short-run fiscal burden on the average U.S. native household of $200, or 0.2 percent of U.S. GDP. In that year, the immigration surplus was about 0.1 percent of GDP. A back-of-the-envelope calculation then suggests that in the short run immigration in the mid-1990s reduced the annual income of U.S. residents by about 0.1 percent of GDP. Given the uncertainties involved in making this calculation, one should not put great stock in the fact that the resulting estimate is negative. The prediction error around the estimate, though unknown, is likely to be large, in which case the 0.1 percent estimate would be statistically indistinguishable from zero. Using this sort of analysis, we cannot say with much conviction whether the aggregate impact of immigration on the U.S. economy is positive or negative. What available evidence does suggest is that the total impact is small.

The Impact of Illegal Immigration

When considering reforms to U.S. immigration policy, it is not the total effect of immigration on the U.S. economy that matters but the impact of the immigrants who would be affected by the changes currently being considered in U.S. admission and enforcement policies. The immigrants that account for the negative fiscal impact of immigration in California and the United States as a whole are primarily individuals with low skill levels. This group includes legal immigrants (most of whom presumably entered the country on family-based immigration visas) and illegal immigrants. The Center for Immigration Studies (CIS), a think tank that advocates reducing immigration, has recently applied the NRC methodology to estimate the fiscal impact of illegal immigration. The CIS finds that in 2002 illegal immigrants on net received $10 billion more in government benefits than they paid in taxes, a value equal to 0.1 percent of U.S. GDP in that year. With unauthorized immigrants accounting for 5 percent of the U.S. labor force, U.S. residents would receive a surplus from illegal immigration of about 0.03 percent of GDP. Combining these two numbers, it appears that as of 2002 illegal immigration caused an annual income loss of 0.07 percent of U.S. GDP. Again, given the uncertainties surrounding this sort of calculation, one could not say with much confidence that this impact is statistically distinguishable from zero.

The net economic impact of immigration on the U.S. economy appears to be modest. Available evidence suggests that the immigration of high-skilled individuals has a small positive impact on the incomes of U.S. residents, while the arrival of low-skilled immigrants, either legal or illegal, has a small negative impact. Given that the estimates in question require strong assumptions and in the end are only a fraction of a percent of U.S. GDP, one cannot say that they differ significantly from zero. For the U.S. economy, immigration appears to be more or less a wash. . . .

The Debate About Specific Consequences

While the aggregate impacts of both legal and illegal immigration are small, the intensity of the public debate about the economic impacts of immigration is not a reflection of its aggregate consequences. Business, which is the biggest winner from high levels of immigration, is the strongest defender of the status quo. Low-skilled workers and select high-skilled workers whose wages are depressed by immigration, at least in the short run, want to see tougher enforcement. Nationally, the less educated tend to be the most opposed to immigration, with their opposition being stronger in states with larger immigrant populations.

While the aggregate impacts of both legal and illegal immigration are small, the intensity of the public debate about the economic impacts of immigration is not a reflection of its aggregate consequences.

Taxpayers in high-immigration states have also been vocal opponents of illegal immigration. States pay most of the costs of providing public services to immigrants, which include public education to immigrant children and Medicaid to poor immigrant households (whose U.S.-born children and naturalized members are eligible to receive such assistance). The federal government, in contrast, appears to enjoy a net fiscal surplus from immigration. Washington is responsible for many activities, including national defense and managing public lands, whose cost varies relatively little with the size of the population. Since immigrants (including many illegals) pay federal income and withholding taxes, the federal government enjoys an increase in revenue from immigration but does not incur much in the way of additional expenses, which are borne primarily at the state and local level. Part of the political opposition to immigration comes from the uneven burden sharing associated with labor inflows. Governors in high-immigration western states, regardless of their party affiliation, have been among the strongest critics of lax federal enforcement against illegal entry.

Results from public opinion surveys bear out this analysis. College graduates, while generally more supportive of immigration, are less supportive in states that have larger populations of low-skilled immigrants and more generous welfare policies, which in combination tend to produce larger tax burdens on high-income individuals.

Illegal Immigrants Drain Health Care Resources

Elizabeth Lee Vliet

Elizabeth Lee Vliet is a women's health specialist and the founder of HER Place: Health Enhancement Renewal for Women Inc.

The national spotlight is on Arizona for doing what the federal government and previous Governor [Janet] Napolitano refused to do: rein in an invasion of illegal aliens bankrupting our state (Arizona). At an August 2009 healthcare Town Hall in Phoenix, legislators said that more than half of Arizona's 4 billion dollar budget deficit was the result of paying for three areas of services to illegal immigrants: education, healthcare, and incarceration.

Uncompensated Healthcare for Illegal Immigrants

What does illegal immigration have to do with your costs and your access to medical care when you need it?

Estimates are that 20–40% of uncompensated ("free") medical services are provided to people in the US illegally. The actual number may be much higher. Shockingly, hospitals and clinics don't ask about citizenship . . . a medical version of "Don't Ask, Don't Tell."

In both Tucson and Dallas where I have practiced medicine, hospitals are struggling under massive costs of uncompensated medical services for uninsured people who, by federal law, cannot be turned away for lack of insurance or ability to pay.

How much does this uncompensated care actually cost taxpayers? The incredible answer: no one knows.

We only have "estimates" of the costs to taxpayers to treat illegal immigrants because hospitals and public health clinics do not ask for proof of citizenship before providing care.

The Effects of Treating Illegal Immigrants

What are the consequences to taxpaying citizens?

1. Increased cost and reduced access to trauma care. Tucson has lost all but one Level I Trauma Center to serve all of southern Arizona, in large part due to massive, unsustainable losses from uncompensated care. Auto accidents involving overloaded vans of illegal aliens happen regularly in southern Arizona. Injured are flown by air ambulance to University Medical Center's Trauma Center and treated with state-of-the-art care . . . all at taxpayer expense.

2. A registered nurse [RN] involved with the Pima County health system since the 1970s who must remain anonymous because of her role, said she has never seen any staff member at either El Rio [Community Health Center] or Pima County Health Department ask for proof of citizenship before providing free medical services (immunizations, well-baby checks, food stamps, WIC [Women, Infants, and Children] services, birth control, and even elective abortions). Costs are paid by taxpayers. When funds are depleted, low-income American citizens have fewer services and longer waits as a result.

3. This same RN also said: "I personally know Mexican men who married 16-year-old girls, got them pregnant, brought them to Tucson for the baby to become a US citizen. They live in Mexico but come here for their health care. Taxpayers pay for this medical care in many ways, at the Public Health Department, and with school nurses who provide care."

4. Uncompensated medical services for illegal immigrants mean higher premiums for all of us due to cost shifting among all third-party payers. To cover the deficits from "free" medical services they provide, the administration at University Physicians Healthcare Kino campus is analyzing how much to increase employee health insurance premiums as of July 1.

5. Obamacare [referring to health care reform laws signed in March 2010] cuts benefits to American citizens: $500 billion in Medicare cuts and slashing the Medicare Advantage program. Medicare Advantage, chosen by one in five seniors, is the most popular plan for low- and moderate-income seniors, and covers about half of our Hispanic or African-American elderly. My patients on Medicare have worked and paid into the system over their working careers, yet these cuts mean less healthcare available to them now. We certainly cannot afford to cover those here illegally.

6. Hospitals in Tucson and Dallas also provide uncompensated ("free") maternity services to pregnant women here illegally. Their babies then become US citizens entitled to all of the services available for low-income American families—food stamps, WIC, immunizations, office visits, medications, etc. This drives up costs to all of us: higher premiums for private insurance companies, and higher taxes for government insurance like Arizona's Medicaid (AHCCCS [Arizona Health Care Cost Containment System]).

7. Professional estimates are that over half of the pregnant women served at Parkland hospital in Dallas are in this country illegally. With over 16,000 deliveries a year, Parkland is one of the nation's busiest maternity services with prenatal clinics for low-income women to receive

free prenatal care, nutrition, medication, birthing classes, child care classes, and free supplies (formula, diapers, bottles, car seats). Taxpayers pay the bills.

Working, taxpaying, legal citizens are bearing the brunt of the failure of our government officials to document citizenship before providing medical services.

A Failure to Document Citizenship

How many of these women are legal citizens and how many are not? No one knows. No one asks about citizenship.

It is significant that the 4 states with the highest number of uninsured patients are the southern border states that also have the highest burden of illegal immigrants: California, Arizona, New Mexico and Texas.

The bottom line is that working, taxpaying, legal citizens are bearing the brunt of the failure of our government officials to document citizenship before providing medical services.

How long before your medical care is delayed or denied because our health systems have collapsed from deficits due to uncompensated medical care?

Arizona's massive deficits, greatly increased by healthcare services for illegals, is the canary in the mine, warning of a potential explosion that may collapse the system for all.

It's straight out of the Cloward-Piven playbook [the Cloward-Piven strategy by sociologists Richard Cloward and Frances Fox Piven]: Destroy the system by overwhelming it. Your state—and your healthcare—may be next.

Illegal Immigration Leads to Higher Crime Rates

Jack Martin

Jack Martin, a retired US diplomat, is director of special projects at the Federation for American Immigration Reform (FAIR).

Most Americans equate illegal aliens with a higher incidence of crime. Some academic researchers have attempted to prove that is a misimpression. But, in fact, data show that the American public understands the facts better than the academics.

Adult illegal aliens represented 3.1 percent of the total adult population of the country in 2003. By comparison, the illegal alien prison population represented 4.54 percent of the overall prison population. Therefore, deportable criminal aliens were nearly half again as likely to be incarcerated as their share of the population.

Misleading Studies on Immigrant Crime

The misleading data produced by academics and think tank researchers that show a lower incidence of crime by aliens is based upon a comparison of data that include all foreign-born residents with data for the native-born population. Because these data compare all foreign-born residents to the native-born population, they are largely irrelevant to describing the illegal alien crime incidence.

A lower incidence of crime should be expected from a foreign-born population that is largely legal immigrants and long-term nonimmigrants. This population includes persons who are screened for any previous criminal activities before they can get a green card, persons who are again screened for criminal activity before they can become U.S. citizens, and persons such as foreign students and professional workers who are at the least required to state under oath whether they have any criminal history before they can get a visa. In other words, this is a population carefully screened to assure that they are unlikely to engage in criminal activity. Something would be very wrong with our visa screening process if research did not reveal that the foreign born were less likely to have committed crimes in the United States than the native-born population.

Deportable criminal aliens were nearly half again as likely to be incarcerated as their share of the population.

The same cannot, of course, be said for the illegal alien population. Their presence in the United States is based on their either illegally entering the country or entering under false pretenses. Those who sneak into the country undergo no form of screening for criminality or any other grounds for exclusion. Many in the illegal alien population end up incarcerated as a result of criminal activity at the time of their illegal entry, e.g. [for example], drug smuggling or alien smuggling. Other illegal aliens owe alien smugglers for assisting their illegal entry and end up being co-opted into criminal activity, such as drug distribution or prostitution, to pay off the debt.

The Pattern of Crime in Arizona

The apparent linkage between illegal alien status and a higher incidence of crime was suggested in the data presented in a recent study of the costs of illegal immigration in Arizona. That study noted that Arizona in 2000 had the highest per capita rate of illegal aliens in the country and also ranked at the top of a number of crime indexes. It had the nation's highest per capita rate of property crimes, the highest rate of vehicle theft, and the 2nd highest rate in the country of larceny theft. For burglaries, it ranked 5th, for murders 9th, and for robberies and aggravated assaults it ranked 15th in the country.

There is nothing about the population in Arizona that would appear to explain this pattern of crime incidence other than the illegal alien population and the proximity to the border with Mexico.

Reliable Data for Illegal Immigrant Crime

To obtain a valid view of the incidence of criminal activity by illegal aliens in comparison to the general population, it is necessary to focus just on that segment of the population. The only data that directly identify criminal illegal aliens depend on resources of the federal government. The federal State Criminal Alien Assistance Program (SCAAP) is administered by the federal government to reimburse states and local jurisdictions for costs incurred for the incarceration of criminal aliens. It offers the only reliable data for a valid assessment of the share of prisoners who are deportable aliens.

In that program, states and local jurisdictions may submit names and records of persons known or believed to be illegal aliens to the Department of Justice. Those records are vetted to eliminate persons who are U.S. citizens and any aliens whose incarceration does not make them deportable. Data reported in the SCAAP reimbursements were used in this study to determine the correlation between the size of the criminal alien population and the noncriminal alien population.

None of these aliens are in prison for simply being illegally in the country unless they illegally reentered after being deported. The vast majority of them will have been convicted of some crime while in the United States. A large share of them will have committed multiple crimes. A U.S. government study reported that, "In our population study of 55,322 illegal aliens, we found that they were arrested at least a total of 459,614 times, averaging about 8 arrests per illegal alien. Nearly all had more than 1 arrest."

Analyzing the Data

Data collected in the SCAAP reporting system were stated in terms of incarceration days. This eliminates any distortion based on length of sentence. Nationwide there were nearly 600 million incarceration days reported, and the number of those days attributable to identified and suspected illegal aliens was about 24.5 million incarceration days. That suggests that one of every 21 prisoners is a deportable alien (4.54%).

The comparison of this prisoner population with the population at large requires identifying a comparable population. Clearly only adults or near adults are likely to be in this population. To obtain an estimate of adult illegal aliens, the INS [Immigration and Naturalization Service] estimates can be used, even though they probably understate the size of that population. To adjust those estimates to a population comparable to an adult population the only available resource is to reduce the INS estimate by an estimate of illegal alien school-age population. The estimate of illegal alien school-age children, done in an earlier study, provides a rough estimate of the K–12 population by state. Because of the age profile of this group, there will be some pre-K illegal aliens and post–grade 12 illegal alien teenagers included in the resulting estimate of a bit more than 7 million illegal aliens in 2000. The comparable adult national population in 2000 is about 230 million persons, and the comparison of these two data sets yields a 2.94 percent share of the adult national population that is composed of illegal aliens, i.e. [that is], one in every 31 residents in the country.

Thus the likelihood that an illegal alien will be among those incarcerated (1 in 21) is significantly greater than the share of adult illegal aliens in the country (1 in 31). It is this greater likelihood of being incarcerated that clearly demonstrates that illegal aliens are disproportionately involved in criminal activity.

The Pattern of Incarceration Nationwide

The data show a clear pattern both nationwide and in the states with the largest estimated illegal alien populations of a higher rate of incarceration of aliens than for the non-alien population. However, the pattern is not uniform. In five of the 13 states with estimated illegal alien populations of over 100,000 in 2000, the reverse was true. Those states were Georgia, Illinois, North Carolina, Texas and Virginia.

Looking at those 13 states as a whole, in 2000 they had about 54 percent of the country's adult population and more than 85 percent of the estimated adult illegal alien population. They also had about 61 percent of the total amount of total criminal incarceration reported in SCAAP and more than 85 percent of the deportable alien incarceration reported in that program.

Illegal aliens are disproportionately involved in criminal activity.

These calculations demonstrate that the rate of incarceration overall was both higher in these 13 states than in the country as a whole and much higher than in the remaining states and the District of Columbia taken together. Nevertheless, in the rest of the country, the average estimated adult illegal alien share was one percent and the related share of the incarcerated illegal alien share was 70 percent larger (1.7%).

The states that had the highest rates of incarcerated aliens above the share of the estimated illegal alien adult population were, in order, New York, Washington, Florida, Arizona, and California. In each of these states, the alien prisoner population represented more than five percent of the total prisoner population, and in California, the share was higher than one in every nine prisoners.

Illegal Immigrants Take American Jobs

Bob Confer

Bob Confer is a columnist focusing on issues of government and economics.

The biggest issue weighing on the minds of Americans is the economy. Recent decreases in factory orders and consumer confidence, coupled with unemployment/ underemployment nearing 16 percent, have many of those fortunate to have a job once again questioning their job security and financial well-being while those who cannot find a job fret over their long-term prospects after more than two years of economic malaise.

Unemployment and Illegal Immigration

Another issue that remains at the forefront of any discussion concerning America's health is illegal immigration. Thanks to Arizona's much-needed and much-welcomed approach to self-preservation in the face of the federal government's failure to secure the border, our citizens debate on a daily basis what needs to be done to address this problem that has haunted us for decades and has, for the second time in the past 25 years, reached its tipping point.

Despite how these two issues dominate the political talk of the day and how different they seem, most people are oblivious to the fact that they are intertwined: High unemployment is not only a result of stressed market factors, but it has also been created—and prolonged—by our illegal immigration problem. Americans are unable to find gainful employment because jobs are being held by non-Americans who have illegally entered our borders unabated and are illegally employed by companies both large and small. The proof for this claim can be found in a simple breakdown of the numbers.

When looking at the details behind the Department of Labor's June [2010] jobs report it can be concluded that there were a total of 17.2 million Americans without a job, that gigantic sum including those identified as "unemployed" by the government as well as those considered to be "marginally attached" to the workforce.

In his July 1 speech about immigration—his first regarding this matter while in office—President Barack Obama said there were 11 million undocumented immigrants in the United States, numbers comparable to Department of Homeland Security estimations. We know this value is likely very low, as many sources on both sides of the issue (those for open borders, those for regulated borders) peg the number of illegal aliens closer to 20 million. ImmigrationCounters.com— which compiles its statistics using data from numerous public and private sources—puts the population at just under 23 million.

High unemployment is not only a result of stressed market factors, but it has also been created—and prolonged—by our illegal immigration problem.

A 2006 report by Catholic Online analyzed the demographics of these transients and noted that 37.5 percent of the then estimated 12 million illegal immigrants were children, meaning 62.5 percent were adults. If those percentages are accurate to this day, which they likely are, that equates to 14.4 million adult aliens.

An Opportunity to Create Jobs

Now, consider what brings the illegals to America. It's the same thing that brought—and brings—countless legal immigrants to our land: jobs. Thanks to opportunity and a quality of life that is unmatched on this planet (a result of the principles of liberty and free markets in action), the USA has become a destination for Latino job seekers who want to stake a claim and better their lives here or send money back home to Mexico and Central American countries to support their kin. That importance for the dollar and the workers' assumption of support for their extended families abroad (not to mention the reward for the risk taken to cross the border and live freely in a land in which they don't belong) probably means that most of the adult illegal immigrants are working within our borders.

If labor and immigration laws were enforced—and amnesty not granted as the Washington establishment would prefer—that would create up to 14.4 million job openings, satisfying a good many of the 17.2 million jobless legal residents of this nation. That would result in an unemployed population as low as 2.8 million Americans, which works out to be an unemployment rate of 1.8 percent, an absurdly low number far below what many economists consider full employment (four to five percent).

The Jobs Held by Illegal Immigrants

Many supporters of amnesty and unchecked immigration will say that such an assumption is unrealistic because the illegals are supposedly doing jobs that Americans won't do. That exaggeration is grossly incorrect for two reasons: One, statistics show otherwise and, two, Americans will work if given the chance. According to ImmigrationCounters.com, the aliens aren't doing only the most menial of chores; 11.7 million of their jobs held are skilled positions (construction, maintenance, and the like). Regarding the remaining jobs (those of the low-skill sort), they would become utilized by the American worker were unemployment insurance to actually follow its predetermined allotments and not be extended at every chance possible by Congress (which forces dependency on government). The unemployed would choose to take the career path (if only temporarily) that they had not previously considered.

It is obvious that in order to straighten out the economy and get more Americans working, government at all levels— local, state, and federal—must focus on the enforcement of existing laws and responsibilities and address the immigration problem in a timely, legal, and effective manner. There's no need to reinvent the wheel and create new legislation because good laws are already there. They're just not being enforced. If state agencies came down hard on the companies that employ illegals and the federal government followed its constitutional obligation to protect the states from invasion, our nation and its economy would get a much-needed boost.

It Is a Myth That Illegal Immigration Leads to Higher Crime Rates

Stuart Anderson

Stuart Anderson is executive director of the National Foundation for American Policy and an adjunct scholar at the Cato Institute.

Recent events in Arizona show how quickly concerns about possible crimes committed by immigrants can dominate the immigration policy debate. The murder of an Arizona rancher in March [2010] became the catalyst for the state legislature passing a controversial bill to grant police officers wider latitude to check the immigration status of individuals they encounter. But do the facts show immigrants are more likely to commit crimes than natives?

Perception vs. Statistics

The situation in Arizona is a classic case of perception becoming more important than statistics. "There is nothing more powerful than a story about a gruesome murder or assault that leads in the local news and drives public opinion that it is not safe anywhere," according to Scott Decker, an Arizona State University criminologist.

In a recent article, Daniel Griswold, director of the Center for Trade Policy Studies at the Cato Institute, writes, "According to the most recent figures from the U.S. Department of Justice, the violent crime rate in Arizona in 2008 was the lowest it has been since 1971; the property crime rate fell to its lowest point since 1966. In the past decade, as illegal immigrants were drawn in record numbers by the housing boom, the rate of violent crimes in Phoenix and the entire state fell by more than 20 percent, a steeper drop than in the overall U.S. crime rate."

National studies have reached the conclusion that foreign-born (both legal and illegal immigrants) are less likely to commit crimes than the native-born.

Griswold notes that in a story in the *Arizona Republic*, the assistant police chief in Nogales, Roy Bermudez, "shakes his head and smiles when he hears politicians and pundits declaring that Mexican cartel violence is overrunning his Arizona border town. 'We have not, thank God, witnessed any spillover violence from Mexico,' Chief Bermudez says emphatically. 'You can look at the crime stats. I think Nogales, Arizona, is one of the safest places to live in all of America.'"

The Immigrant Crime Rate

Data show immigrants are less likely to commit crimes than the native-born, a pattern confirmed by a 2008 study of data from California: "When we consider all institutionalization (not only prisons but also jails, halfway houses, and the like) and focus on the population that is most likely to be in institutions because of criminal activity (men 18–40), we find that, in California, U.S.-born men have an institutionalization rate that is 10 times higher than that of foreign-born men (4.2 percent vs. 0.42 percent). And when we compare foreign-born men to U.S.-born men with similar age and education levels, these differences become even greater," according to research by economists Kristin F. Butcher (Federal Reserve Bank of Chicago) and Anne Morrison Piehl (Rutgers University and the National Bureau of Economic Research). Looking only at prisons, the researchers found, "U.S.-born adult men are in-carcerated at a rate two-and-a-half times greater than that of foreign-born men."

National studies have reached the conclusion that foreign-born (both legal and illegal immigrants) are less likely to commit crimes than the native-born. "Among men age 18–39 (who comprise the vast majority of the prison population), the 3.5 percent incarceration rate of the native-born in 2000 was 5 times higher than the 0.7 percent incarceration rate of the foreign-born," according to the Immigration Policy Center.

Those studying the issue point to logical explanations as to why the crime rate of immigrants is low. "Currently U.S. immigration policy provides several mechanisms that are likely to reduce the criminal activity of immigrants," write Butcher and Piehl. "Legal immigrants are screened with regard to their criminal backgrounds. In addition, all noncitizens, even those in the U.S. legally, are subject to deportation if convicted of a criminal offense that is punishable by a prison sentence of a year or more, even if that is suspended. Furthermore, those in the country illegally have an additional incentive to avoid con-tact with law enforcement—even for minor offenses—since such contact is likely to increase the chances that their illegal status will be revealed."

The Latest Research

In new research published in the June 2010 issue of *Social Science Quarterly*, University of Colorado at Boulder sociologist Tim Wadsworth examined U.S. Census and Uniform Crime Reports data in U.S. cities. Wadsworth notes that one reason to conduct such research was the historical perception that immigrants increase the rate of crime: "The popular discourse surrounding anti-immigrant legislation rests on the assump-tion that encouraging, allowing, or not doing enough to pro-hibit poor, unskilled, and uneducated individuals to immi-grate increases crime rates and the danger of victimization.

Sometimes the concerns focus on all immigration, other times only illegal immigration, and in much of the discourse a clear distinction is not made."

Wadsworth examined U.S. cities with a population of 50,000 or higher and used "cross-sectional time-series models to determine how changes in immigration influenced changes in homicide and robbery rates between 1990 and 2000." The results were clear: "[C]ities with the largest increases in immigration between 1990 and 2000 experienced the largest decreases in homicide and robbery during the same time period. . . . The findings offer insights into the complex relationship between immigration and crime and suggest that growth in immigration may have been responsible for part of the precipitous crime drop of the 1990s."

Wadsworth is not the only researcher to make this connection. He notes that in 2006 Harvard University sociologist Robert Sampson "proposed that not only have immigrants not increased crime, but they may be partly responsible for one of the most precipitous declines in crime that the U.S. has ever experienced." Wadsworth concludes, "The current findings offer empirical support to this claim. Time-series models suggest that the widely held belief that has motivated much of the public and political discourse about immigration and crime is wrong. In contrast, the research offers initial support for the idea that the increase in immigration was partially responsible for the decrease in homicide and robbery in urban areas between 1990 and 2000."

An Unsolved Murder

The murder of Arizona rancher Robert Krentz remains unsolved. It is unclear whether the perpetrator was involved in drug smuggling, human smuggling, born in the U.S. or an illegal immigrant.

In general, we know that illegal immigrants do not exhibit violent resistance when apprehended by U.S. Border Patrol agents. In more than 10 million apprehensions since 2000 we have not seen much evidence of those entering illegally to work in the U.S. arming themselves to fight Border Patrol agents. However, individuals linked to organized crime rings are likely to be armed, given their involvement in drug or human smuggling and the money involved.

In the case of immigration, the lack of temporary work visas and the increased difficulty of entering illegally due to increased enforcement have compelled more illegal immigrants to turn to coyotes—middlemen who guide illegal immigrants across the border to evade the Border Patrol. With the lure of money, criminal gangs have taken over most of the smuggling operations. Illegal immigrants themselves are often victims of these smugglers: Arizona police report increased kidnappings in Phoenix and elsewhere of individuals who are smuggled across the border and then held for ransom.

According to authorities, illegal immigrants have been held for weeks and beaten until a relative can pay ransom beyond the cost of any smuggling fees paid before crossing the border. "[A]s border crossings decline, gangs earn less money directly from smuggling fees than from holding some of their clients for ransom, before delivering them to their destination further inside the U.S.," writes Joel Millman in the *Wall Street Journal.*

The best way to reduce lawlessness along the border is to put in place a work visa law that removes the profits from smugglers.

Years ago, coyotes were small operators often smuggling the same illegal immigrants into the U.S. from year to year. "Now, organized gangs own the people-smuggling trade," writes Millman. "According to U.S. and Mexican police, this is partly an unintended consequence of a border crackdown.

Making crossings more difficult drove up their cost, attracting brutal Mexican crime rings that forced the small operators out of business."

Much of the lawlessness and the violation of the rights of property owners could be eliminated with the introduction of increased legal means of entry for the foreign-born to work in the U.S. Foreign-born workers do not wish to cross hazardous terrain or risk kidnapping at the hands of smugglers any more than an American would. The best way to reduce lawlessness along the border is to put in place a work visa law that removes the profits from smugglers and thereby reduces the risks faced by would-be foreign workers and U.S. property owners.

Taxes Paid by Illegal Immigrants Help Social Security

Edward Schumacher-Matos

Edward Schumacher-Matos is a syndicated editorial writer for the Washington Post Writers Group.

The contributions by unauthorized immigrants to Social Security—essentially, to the retirement income of everyday Americans—are much larger than previously known, raising questions about the efforts in many states and among Republicans in Congress to force these workers out.

In response to a research inquiry for a book I am writing on the economics of immigration, Stephen C. Goss, the chief actuary of the Social Security Administration and someone who enjoys bipartisan support for his straightforwardness, said that by 2007, the Social Security trust fund had received a net benefit of somewhere between $120 billion and $240 billion from unauthorized immigrants.

That represented an astounding 5.4 percent to 10.7 percent of the trust fund's total assets of $2.24 trillion that year. The cumulative contribution is surely higher now. Unauthorized immigrants paid a net contribution of $12 billion in 2007 alone, Goss said.

Previous estimates circulating publicly and in Congress had placed the annual contributions at roughly half of Goss's 2007 figure and listed the cumulative benefit on the order of $50 billion.

The Social Security trust fund faces a solvency crisis that would be even more pressing were it not for these payments.

"If for example we had not had other-than-legal immigrants in the country over the past," Goss e-mailed me, "then these numbers suggest that we would have entered persistent shortfall of tax revenue to cover [payouts] starting [in] 2009, or six years earlier than estimated under the 2010 Trustees Report."

Americans are faced with the difficult choice of cutting pensions, delaying the retirement age or raising taxes if we want to maintain the solvency of what has been the centerpiece of social welfare for ordinary Americans since the 1930s.

Legal immigrants are also net contributors to the pensions of the rest of us because they are relatively young as a group. But the benefit we receive from unauthorized immigrants carries special irony. Immigration restrictionists in Arizona, Virginia, Texas and almost every state in the country are pushing bills and local ordinances to force them out by making it difficult to get jobs, rent apartments, send their children to college or drive cars.

The Social Security actuaries estimate that two-thirds of unauthorized immigrant workers, or 5.6 million people, were paying into the system in 2007.

The Pew Hispanic Center estimated this week that the number of unauthorized immigrants in the country dropped from a peak of 12 million in March 2007 to 11.1 million in March 2009. The drop is due in part to the recession but also to the hostile atmosphere toward unauthorized immigrants.

The Obama administration isn't helping much. Barack Obama, like George W. Bush before him, favors legalizing most of the unauthorized. But in making enforcement systems tighter to curtail future illegal immigration, his administration is deporting ever more of the ones already here—to the tune of 400,000 this year. Yet the administration has resisted pressuring congressional Democrats to craft a legalization bill, in part because of Republican opposition.

Adding to the Social Security irony is that the restrictionists are mostly older or retired whites from longtime American families. The very people, in other words, who benefit most from the Social Security payments by unauthorized immigrants.

The Social Security actuaries estimate that two-thirds of unauthorized immigrant workers, or 5.6 million people, were paying into the system in 2007. Roughly half used a Social Security number tied to an invented name or one that belonged to someone else. Of the rest, many got legal cards when they entered the country under a temporary work visa. They stayed illegally after their visas expired.

About 180,000 unauthorized immigrants received about $1 billion in fraudulent benefits in 2007, Goss said. These benefits are subtracted from the net contribution. Few of the unauthorized workers are likely to receive anything, ever. About the only way they might would be if they were to become legal, and they had paid their withholding taxes using their true names.

The decline in illegal immigration, plus tighter workplace enforcement, means that contributions from the unauthorized will decrease. But as Goss notes, they remain, because of larger families, a positive contributing factor to Social Security solvency.

Somebody ought to say thank you.

CHAPTER 3

Are Current Policies Regarding Illegal Immigrants Working?

Overview: The Evolution of US Immigration Policy

Congressional Budget Office

The Congressional Budget Office provides the US Congress with nonpartisan analyses to aid in economic and budgetary decisions on the wide array of programs covered by the federal budget.

Immigration has been a subject of legislation for U.S. policy makers since the nation's founding. In 1790, the Congress established a process enabling people born abroad to become U.S. citizens. The first federal law limiting immigration qualitatively was enacted in 1875, prohibiting the admission of criminals and prostitutes. The following year, in addressing efforts by the states to control immigration, the Supreme Court declared that the regulation of immigration was the exclusive responsibility of the federal government. As the number of immigrants rose, the Congress established the immigration service in 1891, and the federal government assumed responsibility for processing all immigrants seeking admission to the United States.

The Quota System

During World War I [1914–18] immigration levels were relatively low. However, when mass immigration resumed after the war, quantitative restrictions were introduced. The Congress established a new immigration policy: a national-origins quota system enacted as part of the quota law in 1921 and revised in 1924. Immigration was restricted by assigning each nationality a quota based on its representation in past U.S. census figures. The Department of State distributed a limited number of visas each year through U.S. embassies abroad, and

Congressional Budget Office, *Immigration Policy in the United States*, February 2006.

the immigration service admitted immigrants who arrived with a valid visa. Citizens of other countries could move permanently to the United States by applying for an immigrant visa. Foreign citizens traveling to the United States for a limited time (for instance, foreign exchange students, business executives, or tourists) could apply for a nonimmigrant visa.

Family reunification was a fundamental goal of the quota law of 1921 and the updated quota law of 1924. Those laws favored immediate relatives of U.S. citizens and other family members, either by exempting them from numerical restrictions or by granting them preference within the restrictions. Subsequent laws continued to focus on family reunification as a major goal of immigration policy.

Immigration has been a subject of legislation for U.S. policy makers since the nation's founding.

The Categorical Preference System

The Immigration and Nationality Act of 1965 abolished the national-origins quota system and established a categorical preference system. The new system provided preferences for relatives of U.S. citizens and lawful permanent residents and for immigrants with job skills deemed useful to the United States. However, it did not abolish numerical restrictions altogether. For countries in the Eastern Hemisphere (comprising Europe, Asia, Africa, and Australia), the amendments set per-country and total immigration caps, as well as a cap for each of the preference categories. Although there was a total cap established on immigration from the Western Hemisphere, neither the preference categories nor per-country limits were applied to immigrants from the Western Hemisphere. Immediate relatives of U.S. citizens—spouses, children under 21, and parents of citizens over 21—were exempted from the caps.

The policies established in the 1965 amendments are still largely in place, although they have been modified at various times. In 1976, the categorical preference system was extended to applicants from the Western Hemisphere. In 1978, the numerical restrictions for Eastern and Western Hemisphere immigration were combined into a single annual worldwide ceiling of 290,000. The Immigration Act of 1990 added a category of admission based on diversity and increased the worldwide immigration ceiling to the current "flexible" cap of 675,000 per year. That cap can exceed 675,000 in any year when unused visas from the family-sponsored and employment-based categories are available from the previous year. For example, if only 625,000 people were admitted in 2006, the cap would then be raised to 725,000 for 2007.

The United States also has participated in the resettlement of specific groups of refugees since the close of World War II [1945]. The Refugee Act of 1980 created a comprehensive refugee policy giving the president, in consultation with the Congress, the authority to determine the number of refugees that would be admitted on a yearly basis. It brought U.S. policy in line with the 1967 protocol to the 1951 United Nations [U.N.] refugee convention. The protocol, together with the 1969 Organization of African Unity convention, expanded the number of people considered refugees. The Refugee Act adopted the internationally accepted definition of "refugee" contained in the U.N. Convention and Protocol Relating to the Status of Refugees and applied the same definition to those seeking asylum.

The Issue of Unauthorized Immigration

The Immigration Reform and Control Act of 1986 addressed the issue of unauthorized immigration. It sought to enhance enforcement and to create new pathways to legal immigration. Sanctions were imposed on employers who knowingly hired or recruited unauthorized aliens. The law also created two amnesty programs for unauthorized aliens and a new classification for seasonal agricultural workers. The seasonal agricultural worker amnesty program allowed people who had worked for at least 90 days in certain agricultural jobs to apply for permanent resident status. The legally authorized workers amnesty program allowed current unauthorized aliens who had lived in the United States since 1982 to legalize their status. Under the two amnesty programs, roughly 2.7 million people residing in the United States illegally became lawful permanent residents.

In response to continuing concerns about unauthorized immigration, the Illegal Immigration Reform and Immigrant Responsibility Act of 1996 addressed border enforcement and the use of social services by immigrants. It increased the number of border patrol agents, introduced new border control measures, reduced government benefits available to immigrants, and established a pilot program in which employers and social services agencies could check by telephone or electronically to verify the eligibility of immigrants applying for work or social services benefits.

The Immigration Reform and Control Act of 1986 addressed the issue of unauthorized immigration.

The Homeland Security Act of 2002 created the Department of Homeland Security (DHS) and, in doing so, restructured the Immigration and Naturalization Service (INS), the agency formerly responsible for immigration services, border enforcement, and border inspections. Nearly all functions of the INS were transferred to DHS. Prior law had combined immigrant service and enforcement functions within the same agency; those functions are now divided among different bureaus of DHS. Immigration and naturalization are the responsibility of the Bureau of Citizenship and Immigration Services. The border enforcement functions of the INS are split between two bureaus: the bureau of Customs and Border Protection and the bureau of Immigration and Customs Enforcement.

Current immigration policy offers two distinct ways for noncitizens to enter the United States lawfully: permanent (or immigrant) admission and temporary (or nonimmigrant) admission. People granted permanent admission are formally classified as lawful permanent residents (LPRs) and receive a green card. LPRs are eligible to work in the United States and eventually may apply for U.S. citizenship. Aliens eligible for permanent admission include certain relatives of U.S. citizens and workers with specific job skills, among others. In 2004, the United States admitted about 946,000 people as lawful permanent residents.

Attrition Through Enforcement Is Working to Reduce Illegal Immigrants

Mark Krikorian

Mark Krikorian is executive director of the Center for Immigration Studies, a nonpartisan organization that performs research and analyses on legal and illegal immigration.

Is immigration enforcement effective? Ask the *New York Times*: "Children someday will study the Great Immigration Panic of the early 2000s, which harmed countless lives, wasted billions of dollars and mocked the nation's most deeply held values." An enforcement program that can move the *Times* to such a display of righteous indignation must be doing something right.

The Attrition Strategy

But you don't need to read between the lines to see what's happening on the immigration front. Proof that our belated efforts against illegal immigration are bearing fruit is piling up by the day. Combined federal, state, and local initiatives are demonstrating that the strategy of attrition through enforcement—reducing the illegal population over time, largely through self-deportation rather than mass roundups—actually works.

The headlines tell the story, even if they reliably omit the word "illegal": "Arizona Seeing Signs of Flight by Immigrants," "More Mexicans Leaving U.S. Under Duress," "Hispanics Moving Out of Oklahoma Before New Law Takes Effect," and so on. While the attrition strategy isn't as coordinated as it could be, all levels of government are generally rowing in the same direction. At the federal level, the most notable efforts are directed at denying illegal aliens access to employment, both through stepped-up work site enforcement and through expansion of the voluntary E-Verify system, which enables an employer to check online whether a new hire is eligible to work in the United States. More than 10 percent of all new hires in the nation are already being verified in this way, a percentage that is sure to rise once new rules go into effect requiring that all federal contractors use E-Verify.

> *Combined federal, state, and local initiatives are demonstrating that the strategy of attrition through enforcement . . . actually works.*

They're getting the message in the boardrooms, too. Andersen Windows, for instance, recently performed a personnel audit of employees of a newly acquired firm, resulting in the dismissal of more than 200 illegal aliens. As the Newark *Star-Ledger* put it, such firings "are part of a growing trend in which employers are purging unauthorized workers to avoid a fledgling immigration crackdown by the U.S. government."

State and Local Immigration Enforcement

The approach at the state and local level has become more sophisticated since the 1990s. Then, the major immigration states sued Washington to be reimbursed for the cost of services provided to immigrants, and state efforts were generally directed at limiting access to such taxpayer-funded services. But that didn't work for the simple reason that immigrants— legal or illegal—don't come here just to get welfare. The high rate of welfare use by immigrants (half of all families headed by a Mexican immigrant use at least one major welfare program) is inevitable because, no matter how hard they work, people with very little education or few skills simply cannot earn enough to support their families in the way that our society expects without subsidies from the taxpayer. The federal and state attempts to limit access to welfare, however compelling politically or even morally, failed in the face of the fact that America is not going to let people die on the doorstep of the emergency room simply because they're illegal. What's more, much of the welfare money is spent on the American-born children of illegals, who are U.S. citizens and therefore cannot be denied access to government services.

The most important development we're seeing now at the level of state and local governments is their augmentation of the federal effort to deny jobs to illegals. As of the start of this year [2008] Arizona began requiring all the state's employers to use E-Verify and will revoke the business licenses of firms that persist in knowingly hiring illegal aliens. Other states are also requiring E-Verify for at least some hires, with even the governor of Rhode Island issuing an executive order mandating E-Verify for all state agencies and vendors.

The most important development we're seeing now at the level of state and local governments is their augmentation of the federal effort to deny jobs to illegals.

Another popular effort is what's known in the jargon as a 287(g) program, which gives state or local law enforcement officers extensive training in immigration law and effectively deputizes them as immigration agents. Nearly 50 jurisdictions are participating, with twice that many on the waiting list. The bottleneck is not training the officers, but budgeting for detention space—additional 287(g) programs would turn up more illegals for immigration authorities to take custody of and put somewhere until they're sent home. The effect of such programs is magnified by the fact that, as one writer who's looking into the issue told me, the Spanish-language media hype 287(g) programs and other enforcement initiatives as though they were the Apocalypse, causing illegals to think things are even worse for them than they are.

Evidence of Attrition

School-enrollment statistics provide the first evidence of what blogger Mickey Kaus calls the Gran Salida (Great Exit). Los Angeles, for instance, has seen a 7 percent drop in school enrollment since 2003. Prince William County, Va., which enacted the toughest measures in the Washington, D.C., region, saw a 5 percent drop in English-as-a-second-language enrollment just in the past year. Some illegal aliens and their families are no doubt traveling to other cities or states that are more hospitable to them, with reports of migration from Arizona to Texas, and from Virginia to Maryland. But even this is progress because attrition, in the words of one far-Left critic, is "a strategy aimed at wearing down the will of immigrants to live and work in the United States," and persuading illegals to move to another state can be the first step toward such wearing down.

But they're not all going to other states. A forthcoming report by my colleague Steven [A.] Camarota at the Center for Immigration Studies has found a measurable drop in the total illegal population since last year, with most of them leaving on their own rather than being deported.

The open-borders crowd acknowledges that illegals are leaving, but claims that this development merely buttresses their assertion that immigration is mainly a market-driven phenomenon—when the economy goes sour, illegals go home. Nice try, but there's more to it than that. First, the illegals themselves say otherwise; in the words of one illegal leaving in anticipation of Arizona's tough law, "I don't want to live here because of the new law and the oppressive environment."

An April survey of immigrants from Latin America (half of them illegal) conducted by the Inter-American Development Bank found the same result—28 percent of respondents said they were considering returning home and 81 percent said it was harder to find a job. The role of enforcement came out when respondents were asked whether they considered "discrimination against immigrants" a major problem, and two-thirds said yes. Since that was almost double the proportion who answered yes in a survey in 2001, it's clear that the "discrimination" they're referring to is the enhanced enforcement of the immigration laws, a point reinforced by the fact that illegals were much more likely to point to this "discrimination" than naturalized citizens.

The Need to Keep Up Enforcement

The population data also point in the same direction. While unemployment among illegals has indeed gone up, no doubt contributing to their decisions to leave, the above-mentioned Camarota study finds that the drop in the illegal population has been accompanied by a continuing increase in the legal immigrant population. What's more, the decline in the illegal population seems to have begun with the collapse of the McCain-Kennedy amnesty bill in the Senate, before there was a significant rise in the unemployment rate for illegals. As one Brazilian said of his illegal countrymen in Massachusetts, "When the immigration bill didn't go through, people were very disappointed and started buying tickets [to return home]."

The first priority has to be to prevent the current enforcement push from being discontinued.

There's plenty more to do—we need better marketing for enforcement programs and more funding for state and local police actions, as well as full implementation of the check-in/checkout system at the borders (called US-VISIT) to limit visa overstays, which account for as much as half the illegal population.

But as important as such measures are to accelerating the Gran Salida, the first priority has to be to prevent the current enforcement push from being discontinued by the next president. The success of attrition is an inconvenient truth, as it were, for the amnesty crowd. But since the top immigration priority for both [2008 presidential candidates John] McCain and [Barack] Obama is legalization of the illegal population (McCain told Hispanic officials that "it would be my top priority yesterday, today, and tomorrow"), anything that gets in the way of that goal is a threat.

In the past, spasms of enforcement quickly tapped out, teaching law-breaking businesses and illegal immigrants that they had only to keep their heads down for a time and the storm would pass. Regardless of the election result in November, changing that expectation is essential to regaining control over our immigration system.

State and Local Immigration Enforcement Works and Should Be Expanded

Jessica M. Vaughan and James R. Edwards Jr.

Jessica M. Vaughan is the director of policy studies at the Center for Immigration Studies (CIS). CIS fellow James R. Edwards Jr. is coauthor of The Congressional Politics of Immigration Reform.

Shortly after midnight on September 9, 2001, Maryland state trooper Joseph Catalano pulled over a red Mitsubishi rental car traveling 90 mph in a 65 mph zone on I-95 north of Baltimore. The driver, Ziad Jarrah, had a Florida driver's license and quietly accepted the $270 fine issued by Catalano before continuing on to join his friends at a hotel in New Jersey. Two days later, Jarrah boarded United Airlines Flight 93, which he would later pilot into a field near Shanksville, Pa., killing everyone aboard.

The 287(g) Program

In 2001, Trooper Catalano had no way of knowing that Jarrah was an illegal alien who had overstayed his business visitor visa. But in the years since 9/11 [September 11, 2001, terrorist attacks on the United States], dozens of state and local law enforcement agencies have been able to join ranks with federal immigration authorities under the auspices of the 287(g) program to help identify and remove foreign nationals who commit crimes or otherwise pose a threat to our well-being. These state and local agencies are making a significant contribution to public safety and homeland security, not just in their jurisdictions, but for us all.

Yet the [Barack] Obama administration, in a move consistent with other recent steps to scale back immigration law enforcement, recently announced its intent to impose new rules for the 287(g) program that unduly constrain the local partners and could allow too many alien scofflaws identified by local agencies to remain here. But even with these changes, which seem to be based on unsubstantiated criticism from ethnic and civil liberties groups, the 287(g) program still remains an effective tool in immigration law enforcement and local crime fighting. To ensure its continued success, Congress should provide additional funding and guidance to Immigration and Customs Enforcement (ICE), so that the program continues to meet the needs of local agency partners and the communities they protect. . . .

The Intent of the Legislation

The 287(g) program provides full-fledged immigration officer training to a set of local or state law enforcement officers. While state and local officers have inherent legal authority to make immigration arrests, 287(g) provides additional enforcement authority to the selected officers such as the ability to charge illegal aliens with immigration violations, beginning the process of removal. Under the program, a law enforcement agency agrees to a number of its officers receiving intensive immigration enforcement training, supervision of 287(g) officers by federal agents for immigration enforcement duties, and is assured of federal immigration cooperation and coordination in certain immigration-related enforcement activities.

This measure was largely noncontroversial and unnoticed. Lobbies on all sides of the immigration issue mostly targeted other provisions, such as mandatory employee verification, or entirely parochial concerns. Even many members of Congress not as attuned to the immigration issue were naturally sympathetic to helping state and local law enforcement agencies.

Contrary to recent claims of some opponents, while the removal of criminal aliens was foremost in the minds of the congressional sponsors, 287(g) was never intended to be limited or focused solely on aliens who commit serious crimes. Rather, the legislation was intended to give local law enforcement agencies a tool to help compensate for the federal immigration agency's limitations. . . .

The 287(g) program still remains an effective tool in immigration law enforcement and local crime fighting.

Barriers to Participation in the Program

Interest in 287(g) has skyrocketed in the past several years. Today, nearly 1,000 officers from 67 state or local agencies participate in the program. Eleven new agreements were announced in July 2009, and about 30 are reportedly on the waiting list.

While its growth has been dramatic, the potential for expansion of 287(g) is huge. It has occurred with little encouragement from ICE; in fact, the growth of the program is more due to word of mouth among law enforcement agencies, news media accounts, and pressure from political leaders and community activist groups concerned about crime associated with illegal immigration. For years DHS [Department of Homeland Security] and ICE resisted expanding the program, citing a lack of resources to meet demand and lack of adequate bed space to house the large numbers of removable aliens who would be identified. ICE has contended that some of the agencies that are applying do not really need it, and tried to steer them toward the catch-all ICE-ACCESS [Agreements of Cooperation in Communities to Enhance Safety and Security] program. ICE has further discouraged prospective applicants by dragging out the application and approval process with what are described by applicant agencies as endless, repetitive, unproductive meetings after meetings with Oz-like layers of bureaucrats. In many instances, the only thing that has cut through the red tape and gamesmanship has been the active involvement of congressional representatives.

Organized Opposition to the Program

In addition to the struggle with ICE, local agencies often encounter organized resistance from local activist groups that traditionally oppose immigration law enforcement, such as the ACLU [American Civil Liberties Union] and ethnic advocacy groups. These groups are reinforced by their national counterparts, which have over the years developed an extensive tool kit of how-to manuals and talking points to help local activists try to shoot down proposed 287(g) agreements. Anti-287(g) advocacy extends even to the legislature in Mexico; a member of the Mexican Senate recently denounced the program, calling it a clear violation of the human rights of Mexicans.

Advocates justify these efforts with an array of studies that claim to establish that 287(g) agreements lead to:

- rampant racial profiling, as local law enforcement officers focus on arresting people who appear to be immigrants in order to have them deported;

- roundups of innocent or unfairly targeted immigrants on trumped up or minor local charges;

- a deterioration in public safety overall as immigrants become so fearful of local law enforcement authorities that they will refrain from reporting crimes;

- police distraction from more important crime fighting because they spend too much time on immigration law enforcement.

In addition, 287(g) opponents often cite academic studies claiming that immigrant crime is insignificant and less common than the crimes committed by native-born Americans.

Despite being repeatedly invoked in discussions on 287(g) or immigration law enforcement at the local level, none of these claims holds up under scrutiny, and none is consistent with the actual experience or events in the 287(g) jurisdictions. All agencies we interviewed reported having no complaints filed accusing officers of racial profiling, much less any documented abuses. There have been allegations made by community organizations and politicians in a number of 287(g) jurisdictions but, as reported in a GAO [Government Accountability Office] study, to date there have been no substantiated cases of racial profiling or abuse of immigration authority in any 287(g) location. This should not be surprising, as the 287(g) training emphasizes how to avoid racial profiling. In addition, most U.S. law enforcement officers today are well aware of the sensitivity of this issue, and receive considerable training throughout their careers on how to prevent it.

Local agencies often encounter organized resistance from local activist groups that traditionally oppose immigration law enforcement.

Similarly, no 287(g) agencies have engaged in street sweeps or roundups for the sole purpose of questioning members of the community about their immigration status. All 287(g) operations and activities have been conducted in the context of criminal investigations or arrests, and for legitimate law enforcement purposes. DHS has yet to report on a single instance of a local agency overstepping its bounds or authority. Apparently lacking any actual incidents, opponents such as the ACLU and Catholic Charities have staged outreach events in various parts of the country, including Georgia and Maryland, to encourage individuals to file complaints.

The Offenses Prompting Arrest

While it is true that a significant number of those charged with immigration violations under the 287(g) program were arrested for lesser or nonviolent offenses like minor traffic violations, this is not necessarily a sign that agencies or officers are abusing their authority. Many of the correctional institutions screen all those who end up in jail, and if they are found to be in the United States illegally, generally they are removable. Some are held in custody until the disposition of their local and immigration cases, but many are not. Many are given voluntary departure or released pending an immigration hearing.

While many of those charged with immigration violations came to the attention of law enforcement as a result of a traffic stop or minor crime, because of 287(g) officers are able to complete a thorough screening of the aliens' background by using immigration databases and often find out that quite a few of the so-called minor offenders have prior criminal histories that include more serious offenses. A significant percentage have been deported before, and others have multiple arrests in the same jurisdiction or have fled there from another area.

Even in other ICE programs (as in law enforcement in general) the majority of criminal alien removals result from misdemeanor arrests, not felony arrests. The Costa Mesa, Calif., Police Department, for example, which participates in ICE's Criminal Alien Program (CAP) in lieu of 287(g), provided us with statistics covering 11 months of arrests in 2008. A total of 4,765 adults were booked into the Costa Mesa jail from January to November 2008. The ICE agent assigned to the jail screened 609 foreign-born offenders and placed immigration holds on 309. Of those ordered held pending possible removal, only one-fourth (86) resulted from a felony arrest and three-fourths (223) resulted from a misdemeanor arrest. In Irving, Texas, which also participates in CAP, nearly 12 percent of those arrested were illegal aliens, but only 9 percent of those flagged by ICE screeners were arrested on felony charges at that particular time, while 63 percent were charged with misdemeanors, 16 percent for drunk driving, and 12 percent for driving without a license.

The origins of the "chilling effect" theory are unclear, but hard evidence of the phenomenon is nonexistent in crime statistics, social science research, or real-life law enforcement experience.

The "Chilling Effect" Myth

One of the most common concerns voiced in opposition to 287(g) agreements, and to any form of cooperation between local LEAs [law enforcement agencies] and ICE, is that if local agencies become involved with immigration law enforcement, immigrants in their jurisdiction will become so intimidated and fearful of local authorities that they will refrain from reporting crimes or assisting with investigations, leaving these crimes unsolved, and the perpetrators unpunished. Known as the "chilling effect," this theory is promoted by a number of national advocacy groups, including the Police Foundation, the Major Cities Chiefs [Police] Association, and the International Association of Chiefs of Police.

The origins of the "chilling effect" theory are unclear, but hard evidence of the phenomenon is nonexistent in crime statistics, social science research, or real-life law enforcement experience. National crime statistics show no pattern of differences in crime reporting rates by ethnicity, and the most reliable academic research available, based on surveys of immigrants, has found that when immigrants do not report crimes, they say it is because of language and cultural factors, not because of fear of immigration law enforcement.

As just one example, an analysis of calls for service data from the Collier County [Florida] sheriff's office supports the view of many law enforcement professionals that the "chilling effect" is more of an irrational fear (or a politically motivated invention) than a reality. Collier County consists of several diverse jurisdictions, including North Naples, an area that is largely native-born, and Immokalee, an area with a large immigrant population, both legal and illegal. Over the first year of the county's 287(g) program, calls for service dropped 8 percent county wide—a rate that was consistent with the overall drop in crime that year. Even more important, both North Naples and Immokalee showed the same rate in the drop in calls for service, showing no difference between immigrant and native crime reporting after the program was launched.

An extensive analysis of the effects of the Prince William County, Va., immigration enforcement program, which includes 287(g), reports similar results. Conducted by researchers at the University of Virginia, that study found no significant difference in crime-reporting rates between Hispanics and non-Hispanics after the implementation of the county's immigration enforcement initiatives: "[A]mong those who were victims of a crime that occurred in Prince William, the rates of reporting are nearly identical for Hispanics and non-Hispanics, and are statistically indistinguishable within the survey's margin of error."

An Increase in Communication

While rumors abound of illegal aliens who allegedly refrain from reporting crimes out of fear of deportation, we could find no substantiated cases of crime victims who were removed as a result of having reported crimes to authorities, unless the victims happened to be criminals as well. In fact, immigrants coming forward to report crimes is one of the main ways local LEAs and ICE are able to launch investigations against criminal aliens. However, victims and witnesses to crimes are not targets for immigration law enforcement, and this is repeatedly emphasized by ICE and local LEAs in outreach to immigrant communities.

Says Lt. Wes Lynch, of Whitfield County [Georgia]: "Since starting the 287(g) program at our jail, we have had more communication with the immigrant community, not less." The sheriff has included the Mexican consulate and advocates for the immigrant community in discussing the program. Lynch says that immigrants now approach officers at the jail much more regularly and have assisted in locating criminals. For example, one individual they suspected might be an illegal alien came to the jail to report the return to the community of a drug dealer who had already been removed once before as an aggravated felon, enabling them to prosecute him on criminal immigration charges as a penalty for re-entry. Another community member, a naturalized citizen, came forward after the 287(g) program was launched to report a case of immigration-related marriage fraud.

State and local jurisdictions are, by and large, willing to do their part in immigration enforcement.

The 287(g) training increases local officers' awareness of when they should consider the immigration status of crime victims—not for the purpose of removal, but to access the various special protections available to victims, witnesses, and informants under immigration law. For example, someone who is a victim of a gang crime (or any crime) who happens to be an illegal alien might be needed to testify or otherwise assist in the prosecution of the criminal. If the alien lacks status, he is subject to removal at any time. To ensure that does not happen prematurely, the local agency can work with ICE to arrange special status, temporary or otherwise, until the case is resolved. These tools have proven to be a much more powerful way to encourage cooperation from the immigrant community than non-cooperation or sanctuary policies.

Most agencies with 287(g) programs have active outreach programs in place to help ensure that community leaders understand the goals of the program and how the immigration authorities will be used. Law enforcement managers typically invite representatives of foreign consulates to observe how officers with 287(g) authority carry out their duties, and they report that the consulates are usually satisfied that the program will not be misused. Our research turned up no instances where a foreign consulate tried to block a 287(g) program. The opposition usually comes from local cause groups or branches of national advocacy organizations. One local 287(g) program manager stated that he had invited 287(g) opponents to ride along with his officers to observe operations, but had no takers. All LEA representatives we spoke with agreed that agencies participating in 287(g) should work with community advocates to help them understand that they should not stoke fear in the immigrant community by perpetuating the myth of the "chilling effect." . . .

The 287(g) program has been a welcome addition to U.S. immigration law. It represents the forward thinking of serious lawmakers. The program's success, once congressional advocates helped advance it despite bureaucratic resistance, has been significant. However, the 287(g) program could be much bigger, fine-tuned for greater efficiency and effectiveness, and augmented in ways that represent maturing. 287(g) has achieved the success it has due to sustained commitment from Congress, as well as the administrative branch waking up a bit to that promise. State and local jurisdictions are, by and large, willing to do their part in immigration enforcement. The gains of 287(g) will certainly be lost if the troubling change in congressional priority and ICE's bureaucratic games persist.

State and Local Enforcement of Immigration Laws Results in Abuse

Ann Friedman

Ann Friedman is deputy editor of the American Prospect.

I t's tempting to write off Maricopa County [Arizona] Sheriff Joe Arpaio as just another right-wing hatemonger. Like the Pat Buchanans and Lou Dobbs [conservative political commentators] of the world, he has a large platform, talent for exploiting the racist side of populism, and an all-consuming desire for attention.

So what sets Arpaio apart? Whether we like it or not, he's more than a blowhard. His Arizona county covers 9,000 square miles. It has a population of nearly 4 million. He has 4,000 employees and 3,000 "volunteer posse" members. And although his tactics are under investigation by the Justice Department, he continues to receive financial support from the [Barack] Obama administration.

The 287(g) Program

When it comes to his actions on immigration, the federal policy that empowers him is the 287(g) provision, which essentially allows local police and sheriffs to act as national security officials. This "partnership" with the office of [U.S.] Immigration and Customs Enforcement (ICE) has enabled Arpaio to turn his law enforcement bureau into a racial-profiling and immigrant-hunting unit. ICE brags that, through 287(g), local police have identified more than 100,000 "potentially removable aliens."

But in the 66 local police departments that participate in the 287(g) program, there is evidence that actual crime fighting is suffering because of the focus on immigration enforcement. Several prominent police chiefs have called for 287(g) to be repealed. Not only does the program push them to investigate the citizenship status of every person who appears to be Hispanic, it deters undocumented immigrants from reaching out to authorities when they are victims of or witnesses to crime. Police officers' core mission may be to ensure public safety, but 287(g) sends the message that the mission doesn't extend to Hispanics. "How can you police a community that will not talk to you?" one participating police chief asks, in a report on 287(g) by the Police Foundation. And since all the time spent checking documents is time not spent on other law enforcement priorities, everybody loses—not just the Hispanics who are profiled.

ICE officials have said the program is designed to target "serious criminal activity." But a Government Accountability Office [GAO] report on 287(g) released earlier this year [2009] found that in more than half of the 29 jurisdictions it investigated, officers expressed concerns that 287(g) was being used to deport immigrants who had only committed minor crimes, such as traffic violations. Along with local advocacy groups, it called on the federal government to amend the program.

> *The 287(g) program pushes those who are on the margins of our society even further out.*

A Change to the Program

Perhaps in response to the GAO's call for stricter regulation of 287(g) partners, in July, Homeland Security Secretary Janet Napolitano announced changes to the program that were decried both as an expansion of the program (by immigrant rights advocates) and a limitation of it (by deportation hawks). ICE added another 11 jurisdictions to its list of partners and also a requirement that police pursue all charges on which they detain immigrants, a change designed to deter them from deporting those with minor infractions. "This new agreement supports local efforts to protect public safety by giving law enforcement the tools to identify and remove dangerous criminal aliens," Napolitano said.

She should know better. As the former governor of Arizona, Napolitano and Arpaio go way back. Arpaio, one of the most popular politicians in the state, gave Napolitano a boost when he endorsed her 2002 run for governor. And for most of her time in office, she looked the other way as he overstepped his bounds. During her final months as governor, she diverted some state funds from his office, but she never spoke out against his tactics.

Local Enforcement in Practice

In the best possible scenario—the one that ICE touts in its press release—287(g) would merely enable local police to conduct screenings at jails to determine if those already in custody for serious crimes are undocumented immigrants. But Arpaio's actions are a glimpse of how 287(g), in practice, often leads to racial profiling, rather than deportation of dangerous criminals. A recent *New Yorker* profile of Arpaio describes him conducting raids on towns with a high percentage of Hispanic residents. And his chief of enforcement bragged to the *New York Times* last year [2008] that most deputies in Maricopa "can make a quick recognition on somebody's accent, how they're dressed."

The 287(g) program pushes those who are on the margins of our society even further out. But even if Napolitano doesn't care about the rights of Hispanics—or, in Maricopa at least, brown-skinned people wearing clothing styles common in Mexico—she should care about the crime ignored as cops conduct immigration sweeps. As long as Napolitano allows ICE to continue its partnership with jurisdictions like Arpaio's, she's jeopardizing the very security she's supposed to protect.

Current Policies Regarding Illegal Immigrant Children Are Inadequate

Roberto G. Gonzales

Roberto G. Gonzales is assistant professor at the University of Washington School of Social Work.

The current political debate over undocumented immigrants in the United States has largely ignored the plight of undocumented children. About 56 percent of all undocumented immigrants are from Mexico, 22 percent from other nations in Latin America, 13 percent from Asia, 6 percent from Europe and Canada, and 3 percent from Africa and other regions of the world. The children who are part of this undocumented population have, for the most part, grown up in the United States and received much of their primary and secondary educations here as well. About 65,000 undocumented children who have lived in the United States for five years or longer graduate from high school each year. But without a means to legalize their status, these children are seldom able to go on to college, cannot work legally in this country, and cannot put their educations and abilities to the best possible use. This wasted talent imposes financial and emotional costs not only on undocumented students themselves, but on the U.S. economy and U.S. society as a whole.

Undocumented Immigrant Children

These children, born abroad yet brought at an early age to live in the United States by their parents, are among those youth referred to in academic literature as the 1.5 generation be-

Roberto G. Gonzales, "Wasted Talent and Broken Dreams: The Lost Potential of Undocumented Students," *Immigration Policy In Focus*, vol. 5, October 2007. Copyright © 2007. Reproduced by permission of the author.

cause they fit somewhere between the first and second generations. They are not of the first generation since they did not choose to migrate, but neither do they belong to the second generation because they were born and spent part of their childhood outside of the United States. While they have some association with their countries of birth, their primary identification is affected by experiences growing up as Americans. They at times straddle two worlds and are often called upon to assist their parents in the acculturation and adaptation process. Members of the 1.5 generation tend to be bicultural and most are fluent in English. This gives them an advantage in the global economy since they are equipped with bilingual and bicultural skills, which are assets at any level.

However, the experiences of undocumented children belonging to the 1.5 generation represent dreams deferred. Many of them have been in this country almost their entire lives and attended most of their K–12 education here. They are honor roll students, athletes, class presidents, valedictorians, and aspiring teachers, engineers, and doctors. Yet, because of their immigration status, their day-to-day lives are severely restricted and their futures are uncertain. They cannot legally drive, vote, or work. Moreover, at any time, these young men and women can be, and sometimes are, deported to countries they barely know. They have high aspirations, yet live on the margins. What happens to them is a question fraught with political and economic significance.

Currently, education and immigration policies send mixed signals to undocumented students.

This report draws on extensive interviews with Hispanic undocumented young adults in the Los Angeles area and places their experiences in the context of U.S. educational and economic trends and immigration policies. Based on this research, it is evident that—at a time when the supply of available workers in the United States, especially highly skilled workers, is not meeting the demands of the U.S. labor market—providing undocumented students with opportunities to pursue a higher education and to work legally in this country would benefit U.S. taxpayers and the U.S. economy as a whole. This is true not only for the Hispanic undocumented children who are the focus of this report, but also the undocumented children from Asia, Africa, and elsewhere whose talents and potential remain largely untapped as well.

Legal Contradictions and Wasted Talent

Currently, education and immigration policies send mixed signals to undocumented students. As the law now stands, undocumented students can legally go to high school and can legally attend most colleges. The Supreme Court ruled in *Plyler v. Doe* (1982) that, because these children are "persons" under the Constitution and thus entitled to equal protection under the law according to the 14th Amendment, they cannot be denied access to public elementary and secondary education on the basis of their legal status. This decision has enabled thousands of undocumented students to graduate from high school each year.

Nevertheless, once undocumented students graduate from high school and attempt to go to college, the limitations of their legal status become more acute and barriers multiply. Without financial aid, it is extremely difficult to afford a public university. There are a limited number of available scholarships and some aid at a handful of private colleges, but scholarships are too few and tuition at private schools is often much higher than at public universities. Given the numerous barriers to their continued education, and their exclusion from the legal workforce, many undocumented students are discouraged from applying to college. It is estimated that only between 5 and 10 percent of undocumented high school graduates go to college.

This growing pool of young adults who lack adequate educational access or the legal right to work in the United States presents serious problems not only for themselves but for U.S. society as a whole. Whether it is fair or not to make special legal concessions to children who did not have much (or any) say in the decision their parents made to come to or stay in this country without authorization depends on one's philosophical stance. What does not belong to the ephemeral realm of polemics is the fact that the initial investment in their education pays relatively few economic dividends as long as they are limited in their ability to continue on to college and obtain higher-skilled (and higher-paying) jobs that require more than a high school diploma.

Legal Status Pays Economic Dividends

Research indicates that when given an opportunity to regularize their status, undocumented immigrants experience substantial upward mobility. For instance, studies of undocumented immigrants who received legal status under the 1986 Immigration Reform and Control Act (IRCA) have found that, over time, legalized immigrants moved on to significantly better jobs. Similarly, the U.S. Department of Labor found that the wages of immigrants legalized under IRCA had increased by roughly 15 percent five years later. It is therefore likely that if currently undocumented students were granted legal status, they would not only improve their own circumstances but, in turn, make greater contributions to the U.S. economy. Given the opportunity to receive additional education and training, and move into better paying jobs, legalized immigrants pay more in taxes and have more money to spend and invest.

Concurrently, as a result of long-term structural trends in the U.S. economy, having postsecondary education is no longer a luxury but a must for anyone who wishes to successfully compete in today's labor market and command a living wage.

With every step up the degree ladder, workers gain in salary and employment opportunities. According to the Bureau of Labor Statistics (BLS), workers who lacked a high school diploma in 2006 earned an average of only $419 per week and had an unemployment rate of 6.8 percent. In contrast, workers with a bachelor's degree earned $962 per week and had an unemployment rate of 2.3 percent, while those with a doctorate earned $1,441 and had an unemployment rate of only 1.4 percent.

Spending money on the education of Hispanic and immigrant children represents an investment that is recouped by taxpayers.

While the U.S. economy increasingly rewards those with higher education, disparities in the education levels and incomes of Americans persist along the lines of ethnicity and race, with Hispanics and blacks on the lower end and non-Hispanic whites and Asians on the upper end. This continuing trend represents a significant public-policy challenge. Consider the following: Hispanics contributed more than one-third of the increase in the population of 15–19-year-olds between 1990 and 2000 and accounted for one in five new entrants into the national labor force in 2000. Barring unforeseen events, demographic trends—such as falling fertility rates among non-Hispanic women, higher fertility rates among Hispanic women, and continued immigration from Latin America—ensure that the health of the economy will depend on the skills and knowledge of both foreign-born and native-born Hispanic workers. Giving undocumented students (most of whom are Hispanic) the opportunity to pursue a higher education and move up the career ladder would boost the economic potential of the Hispanic population as a whole, and thus the U.S. economy as well. Conversely, denying this opportunity to undocumented students would send precisely the wrong message to Hispanics about the value of a college education—and the value that U.S. society places on their education—at a time when raising the educational attainment of the Hispanic population is increasingly important to the nation's economic health.

An Investment for the Entire Country

A 1999 RAND [Corporation] study found that, although raising the college graduation rate of Hispanics to the same level as that of non-Hispanic whites would increase spending on public education (by about 10 percent nationwide and 20 percent in California), these costs would be more than offset by savings in public health and welfare expenditures and increased tax revenues resulting from higher incomes. For instance, a 30-year-old Mexican immigrant woman with a college degree will pay $5,300 more in taxes and cost $3,900 less in government expenses each year compared to a high school dropout with similar characteristics.

As the RAND study suggests, spending money on the education of Hispanic and immigrant children represents an investment that is recouped by taxpayers. Conversely, the scale of population growth among the Hispanic and immigrant populations compounds the economic importance of their educational attainment. According to the U.S. Census Bureau, for example, Hispanics accounted for half of U.S. population growth between 2000 and 2004, although they comprised 14 percent of the population. By contrast, non-Hispanic whites made up only 18 percent of the increase in population over the same period, though they comprised more than two-thirds of the total population. While the expansion of the Hispanic population was due primarily to immigration in the 1980s and 1990s, births are now outpacing immigration and will increasingly become the most important component of their growth. Between 2000 and 2004, Hispanics accounted for 3.7 million births and net immigration of 2.7 million. Given such growth, an undereducated Hispanic population has implications not only for their own collective mobility, but also for that of the entire country.

The economic importance of immigrant workers is magnified further by long-term demographic trends in the United States. According to BLS projections, the U.S. labor force is expected to grow by 13 percent between 2004 and 2014, from 145.6 million to 164.5 million. However, despite an absolute increase, the rate of labor force growth has been declining over the last two decades as fewer native-born workers become available to join the labor force with every birth cohort. Immigration helps the economy to overcome this demographic challenge. In fact, the immigrant share of the nation's labor force has tripled from 5 percent in 1970 to nearly 15 percent in 2005. Moreover, immigrant workers accounted for 49 percent of total labor force growth between 1996 and 2000, and as much as 60 percent between 2000 and 2004. According to some estimates, immigrants and their children together will account for the entire growth of the U.S. labor force between 2010 and 2030. . . .

The DREAM Act

Undocumented students represent an untapped potential source of the high-skilled workers who are in such demand in California and the nation as a whole. Unfortunately, Congress has yet to unlock the economic potential of these largely U.S.-educated youngsters by allowing them to apply for legal status. However, a bipartisan solution to the current dilemma has been repeatedly introduced and debated in Congress since 2001—so far, without success: the Development, Relief, and Education for Alien Minors (DREAM) Act. The DREAM Act includes provisions enabling undocumented students to obtain legal permanent resident status. According to current immigration law, immigrant children derive their legal status from that of their parents and have no right to legal permanent residency through any other mechanism. In contrast, the DREAM Act would authorize cancellation of removal and adjustment of status for undocumented children if they satisfy the following conditions: (1) entered the United States before age 16; (2) have been continuously present in the country for five years prior to the bill's enactment; (3) have obtained a high school diploma or its equivalent; and (4) demonstrated good moral character.

Undocumented students who satisfy the above conditions would be able to apply for a six-year "conditional" legal permanent status that would allow them to work, go to school, and join the military (provided that they also pass a background security check). If, within this six-year period, the DREAM Act beneficiaries complete at least two years toward a four-year college degree, graduate from a two-year college, or serve at least two years in the U.S. armed forces, they would be able to adjust from conditional to permanent status. The DREAM Act would help to move a million undocumented students out of the shadows and onto a pathway towards legal status and eventual U.S. citizenship. Estimates suggest that the DREAM Act would provide 360,000 undocumented high school graduates with a legal means to work, and could provide incentives for another 715,000 youngsters between the ages of 5 and 17 to finish high school (in order to fulfill the act's eligibility requirements) and pursue postsecondary education.

> *Undocumented students represent an untapped potential source of the high-skilled workers who are in such demand in California and the nation as a whole.*

One particular concern that has been voiced about the DREAM Act is that it could take away seats in colleges and universities, as well as financial aid, from native-born students who want to pursue postsecondary education. However, this fear is not borne out by the experiences of the ten states which, since 2001, have passed laws allowing undocumented students who attend and graduate from in-state high schools to qualify for in-state college tuition. These states (Texas, California, Utah, Washington, New York, Oklahoma, Illinois, Kansas, New Mexico, and Nebraska) are home to about half of the nation's undocumented immigrants. Two of these—New Mexico and Texas—also allow undocumented students to compete for college financial aid, providing a small but significant minority of them with the opportunity to move on to postsecondary education. Such legislation has not precipitated a large influx of new immigrant students, displaced native-born students, or been a financial drain on the educational system. In fact, these measures tend to *increase* school revenues by bringing in tuition from students who otherwise would not be in college. . . .

A Wise Investment

Undocumented students who qualify for legal status under the conditions of the DREAM Act must successfully compete with their peers in high school to earn recognition as top students. They also must successfully compete in the college application process to earn their spots in school. These students are not being given any special allowances to get into college. In fact, many have already done so in spite of very unfavorable conditions and a great many legal and financial barriers. Finally, those who do get into college must compete for financial aid, be it need based or merit based, along with all other students. In other words, the DREAM Act would simply provide undocumented students with the legal right to pursue opportunities they have already earned for themselves. It also would represent an acknowledgement of the fact that encouraging more Hispanics to attend college and join the skilled workforce is an investment in the future of the U.S. economy.

Undocumented students in the United States are currently trapped in a legal paradox. They have the right to a primary and secondary education and are generally allowed to go on to college. But their economic and social mobility is severely restricted due to their undocumented status. The DREAM Act, which would provide a path to legal residence for undocumented youth, is one way out of this legal tight-spot. There is compelling evidence that Congress needs to address the uncertain situation of these hundreds of thousands of young people who are hostages of a confusing and contradictory system. Besides the moral and humanitarian reasons for doing so, there are also strong economic considerations such as ensuring that the investment already made in the schooling of these students is not wasted and that the country is not deprived of productive, educated, and U.S.-trained workers.

Numerous studies demonstrate that legal status brings fiscal, economic, and labor-market benefits to individual immigrants, their families, and U.S. society in general. Over time, given a chance, young men and women who are now undocumented will improve their educations, get better jobs, and pay more in taxes. Given their relatively small numbers, they will make up only a tiny fraction of the total college population and the U.S. workforce as a whole and will not "displace" other students or workers. Yet they could contribute significantly to the growth of the higher-skilled labor force in the years to come. In school we encourage our students to aspire, yet we deny undocumented students the opportunity to share in the "American Dream." Can we really afford to waste such a valuable national resource?

CHAPTER 4

How Should the Government Respond to Illegal Immigration?

Overview: Americans' Views on Immigration Reform Policy

Lydia Saad

Lydia Saad is senior editor at Gallup, one of the world's oldest and most widely recognized public opinion survey firms.

As President Barack Obama renews his call for a comprehensive approach to addressing illegal immigration, Americans are about equally divided—50% to 45%—over whether the government's main focus should be on halting the flow of illegal immigrants coming into the U.S., or on developing a plan to deal with those already here.

Americans' Views on Illegal Immigration

The latest results come from a June 11–13 [2010] *USA Today/Gallup* poll following several months of public discourse over Arizona's new immigration law. In the same poll, by 62% to 32%, Americans are more likely to believe illegal immigrants are a burden on taxpayers by virtue of the social services they receive, rather than people who become productive citizens and eventually contribute their fair share of taxes.

Americans' current attitudes on both questions are similar to June 2006, a month after President George W. Bush delivered an Oval Office address calling on Congress to pass a comprehensive immigration reform bill.

Currently rank-and-file Republicans and Democrats differ significantly in their opinions about which aspect of immigration reform should be the priority. More than two-thirds of Republicans want the government's main focus to be on halting the flow of illegal immigrants, while 55% of Democrats want it to be on dealing with illegal immigrants already in the country. Still, this partisan divide is not quite as strong as has been seen over the past year for other issues such as health care reform, labor organizing, and oil drilling.

At the same time, the plurality, if not majority, of all three political parties believe illegal immigrants cost taxpayers more than they contribute to the tax rolls.

Americans are clearly concerned about the illegal immigration problem.

Seriousness of Concern About Illegal Immigration

Illegal immigration is positioned fairly high as a public concern on two additional Gallup questions included in the latest poll. At 5%, it receives fewer spontaneous mentions from Americans as the nation's "most important problem" than the economy, unemployment, Gulf [Coast] oil disaster, poor leadership, health care, and the federal budget deficit. However, it scores higher than the environment, education, crime, and a host of other issues.

Similarly, in a separate question, the 64% of Americans rating illegal immigration as an "extremely serious" or "very serious" problem is less than the serious ratings for the federal debt, terrorism, health care costs, and unemployment. However, it essentially ties U.S. military involvement in Afghanistan and Iraq and leads the environment, government power, corporate power, and discrimination against minorities issues.

Eight in ten Republicans (79%) compared with half of independents (51%) consider illegal immigration an extremely or very serious threat.

Americans are clearly concerned about the illegal immigration problem. To succeed in addressing the issue, however, policy makers may need to be aware that Americans want to see at least as much emphasis on sealing the border as on addressing the status of current illegal residents. Any bill that is perceived as leaning too far in either direction is bound to produce a political backlash.

Illegal Immigrants Should Not Be Allowed Amnesty

Zach Swartz

Zach Swartz is an intern for Republican US Representative from Pennsylvania Bill Shuster and former government relations associate for the Federation for American Immigration Reform.

With the recent official unemployment rate of 10.2 percent, American workers are now facing the worst job market in 25 years. In fact, over the past 60 years, the unemployment rate has rarely been as high as it is today [November 2009]. Despite a difficult job market, President [Barack] Obama and leaders in Congress are talking about passing so-called "comprehensive immigration reform" legislation. This legislation would give amnesty to 12 million or more illegal aliens, including an estimated 8.3 million illegal aliens who hold jobs they never should have had, and could include a proposed new guest-worker provision to import hundreds of thousands of additional foreign workers. If enacted, illegal aliens would be allowed to keep these jobs instead of making them available to American citizens and legal immigrants who are out of work. Congress has a responsibility to ensure that the law that requires available jobs to be filled by legal workers is respected. Consideration of amnesty, particularly in these harsh economic times, constitutes a failure by Congress to live up to its basic responsibilities to the American people.

The American Job Market

American workers are struggling. The number of available jobs continues to shrink. Today, 15.4 million Americans are out of work and looking for a job and millions more are in temporary part-time jobs while they look for permanent jobs. At the same time, it is estimated that 8.3 million illegal aliens are part of the American workforce despite not being legally authorized to work in the United States. In just the past year, 4.9 million jobs have been lost.

For months, leaders in Congress have been telling the American people that the U.S. economy is facing significant challenges. For example, during debate on President Obama's $800 billion stimulus bill, Senator Charles Schumer (D-N.Y.) said that "the country is in tough shape. We have had the most difficult economic time since the Great Depression." Since he made that remark in February, the economy and the job situation have continued their downward spiral. While today's official 10.0 percent unemployment rate is nowhere near as bad as the 24.8 percent seen in 1933 during the depths of the Great Depression, the current employment picture is the worst Americans have seen in the past 25 years. . . .

Over the past 61 years, American workers have faced an unemployment rate as high as it is today in just 11 out of the past 743 months. . . .

American workers are now facing the worst job market in 25 years.

Since January 1948, unemployment has exceeded the current unemployment rate of 10.0 percent in just two periods: October 1982 to April 1983. Put in historic perspective, today's workers are facing an unemployment rate that has rarely been seen since World War II. The job market presents significant challenges for those Americans who are out of work and looking for a job.

The Consideration of Amnesty

Despite the jobless picture, Senator Schumer, who recently compared today's economy to that of the Great Depression,

135

chaired a hearing several months ago entitled "Comprehensive Immigration Reform in 2009, Can We Do It and How?" The hearing was held on April 30, 2009, before the Senate Judiciary Committee, Subcommittee on Immigration, Refugees and Border Security. Critics say that so-called "comprehensive" reform is a euphemism for legislation that would grant amnesty to 12 million illegal aliens and that this hearing was the first step towards consideration of amnesty in the 111th Congress.

While it comes as no surprise that Schumer would push amnesty, since he has supported it in the past, it is surprising that Congress would even consider amnesty given the current economic climate. Even people from Schumer's own state of New York recognize the reality that pushing amnesty with today's job market is unwise. For example, Rogan Kersh, a dean at New York University's Wagner Graduate School of Public Service, has stated that "rising unemployment rates, coupled with continuing dismal economic news, are battering the public's inclination to back a change in illegal immigrants' status, which was never that strong to begin with."

Underlying Dean Kersh's comment is the fact that the American people intuitively understand that amnesty legislation would authorize illegal aliens to stay in the United States and allow them to keep jobs they should never have had in the first place. The American people understand that, rather than granting amnesty, Congress and the administration should focus on immigration enforcement, which would progressively make available to legal American workers those jobs currently held by illegal aliens. Despite the lack of available jobs for legal American workers and the support of the American people for immigration law enforcement, Senator Schumer has said he will be undeterred by "difficult economic conditions" and will press ahead with the hearing, noting that there is "a real chance of passing comprehensive reform this year."

The 2007 Amnesty Debate

When Congress last considered amnesty in May and June 2007, some politicians suggested that illegal aliens were doing jobs that no Americans would do. That was not true then, and it certainly is not true today. Rep. Steve King (R-Iowa) has made just that point, saying that amnesty supporters "are going to have to be faced with the argument that I and many others are making: Illegals are taking jobs Americans now want." Amnesty would allow an estimated 8.3 million illegal aliens to keep the jobs they currently hold, even though they never should have been hired for those jobs in the first place. In addition, amnesty would allow anyone who is illegally present in the United States to openly begin applying for any and every available job in America. This would put American workers in the position of having to openly compete with (former) illegal aliens to fill an available job. American workers shouldn't have to do that, but amnesty would force them to.

Real enforcement and a reduction in immigration levels would ensure that America restores the integrity of its labor market.

The last time Congress rejected amnesty, in May and June 2007, America's economy was in much better shape than it is today. At that time, big business interests supported amnesty and President [George W.] Bush's guest-worker program, which would have brought in hundreds of thousands of guest workers each year. If the job market could not support those policies in 2007, there is no doubt that the current lack of available American jobs means that America simply cannot support these policies today. . . .

During the 2007 amnesty debate, official unemployment (seasonal) stood at 4.6 percent—4.4 full points lower than the current 10.0 percent. . . . In June 2007, nearly 7.0 million

Americans were out of work, compared to 15.4 million today. In November 2009, 8.5 million more Americans are out of work and actively looking for a job than were in 2007.

The Number of Unemployed

During the last amnesty debate, the number of unemployed Americans declined by 139,000 during the year prior to the debate (comparing July 2006 to June 2007). Over that same one-year period, the unemployment rate had declined slightly from 4.7 to 4.6 percent. By comparison, America has had a net loss of nearly 5 million jobs during the previous one-year period (November 2008 to November 2009) and unemployment has increased by 3.2 percentage points. These numbers translate to a significantly higher number of Americans who are out of work today than were in 2007 (8.5 million more Americans) and suggests that America simply does not need more foreign workers, whether through amnesty, legalization or a guest-worker program. In fact, real enforcement and a reduction in immigration levels would ensure that America restores the integrity of its labor market which would increase wages and free jobs for American workers.

The unemployment numbers also demonstrate that regardless of gender, race, age or education, the employment prospects for all Americans are worse today than they were in June 2007.... Women and men are both facing higher unemployment. In 2007, the unemployment rate for women stood at 3.9 percent; today it is 7.9 percent. Men also face higher unemployment. Unemployment was 4.1 percent for men in 2007 and is now 10.5 percent.

Regardless of race or national origin, Americans across the board are living with employment prospects today that are much worse than in 2007. According to the Bureau of Labor Statistics (BLS), white unemployment is up 5.2 percentage points (from 4.1 to 9.3 percent), Hispanic unemployment is up 7.1 percentage points (from 5.6 to 12.7 percent), and unemployment for African Americans is up 7.1 percentage points (from 8.5 to 15.6 percent). Immigrant unemployment—mostly legal workers—in the first quarter of 2009 was even higher, i.e. [that is], 9.7 percent—the highest level since 1994, when data began to be collected for immigrants. Similarly, the teenage unemployment rate, having risen from 16.1 percent in June 2007 to 26.7 percent in November 2009, is also considerably higher. The teenage unemployment rate for African Americans, at 49.4 percent, is even higher than the national average for all teenagers.

As with other demographics, job losses have hit Americans hard regardless of their level of educational attainment. According to BLS, workers over the age of 25 who have earned a college degree or higher have seen their unemployment rate more than double from 2.0 percent in June 2007 to 4.9 percent in November 2009. The unemployment rate for people with some college but without a degree has more than doubled from 3.6 percent to 9.0 percent, from June 2007 to November 2009.

Amnesty would force those Americans out of work and looking for a job to compete with today's illegal aliens for the limited number of jobs.

The Hardest Hit American Workers

The hardest hit, however, are those Americans older than 25 with "less than a high school diploma." These Americans have seen their demographics' unemployment climb from 6.8 percent to 15.0 percent, from June 2007 to November 2009. Those with a high school diploma but no college have seen unemployment increase from 4.2 percent to 10.4 percent. These numbers represent 1.8 million unemployed Americans without a high school diploma, and 3.9 million more with a high school diploma but no college.

According to the Pew Hispanic Center, illegal aliens are "especially likely to hold low-skilled jobs" because they are "disproportionately likely to be poorly educated." According to Pew research, nearly half of all illegal aliens (47 percent) aged 25 to 64 have "less than a high school education," compared to 8 percent of U.S.-born residents in that age group who have not graduated from high school. Americans who dropped out of high school or completed high school but never attended college will necessarily have to compete in the job market with any illegal alien who receives amnesty and anyone admitted under a new "no skill/low skill" guest-worker program. Americans with no more than a high school diploma, including 5.7 million Americans who are currently unemployed, are the most likely to be economically disadvantaged and are also most likely to be the hardest hit by amnesty or by a guest-worker program.

America's unemployment numbers, taken as a whole, demonstrate an alarming trend for American workers. Unemployment is much higher today—across all demographics and regardless of gender, race, age or education level—than it was the last time Congress considered amnesty in June 2007. Amnesty would force those Americans out of work and looking for a job to compete with today's illegal aliens for the limited number of jobs. The jobless numbers suggest that American workers cannot afford a guest-worker program and that American taxpayers cannot afford amnesty for millions of illegal aliens who would then become eligible for unemployment benefits. Despite this reality for the American worker, Congress has begun holding hearings on amnesty. But the conclusion is unavoidable: If consideration of amnesty was "ripe" in 2007, by today's standards it is simply "rotten."

A Border Fence Is a Good Solution to Illegal Immigration

Jim DeMint

Jim DeMint is a Republican US senator from South Carolina.

There's been a lot of hand-wringing over Arizona's attempt to enforce our nation's immigration laws but not much information about how the federal government has dropped the ball.

The Border Fence

Four years ago [2006], legislation to build 700 miles of double-layer border fence along the southern border was supported by then Sen. Barack Obama and signed into law by President [George W.] Bush. Yet, only a fraction of that fencing is in place today.

According to staff at the Department of Homeland Security (DHS), only 34.3 miles of double-layer fencing has been completed along the southern border. Most of that fencing, 13.5 miles, is in Texas, while 11.8 miles are in California and 9.1 miles of double-layer fencing are up in Arizona.

The lack of double-layer fencing can be traced to a 2007 amendment that eliminated the double-fencing requirement and allowed the DHS the option to put other types of less effective fencing in its place. It was lumped into a massive, omnibus-spending bill that President Bush signed into law on December 26, 2007.

That's when construction on the double-layered fence essentially stopped. The Government Accountability Office (GAO), Congress's investigative arm, reported in early 2009 that only 32 miles of double-layer fencing had been built. That means under President Obama, only 2.3 miles of it has been built over an entire year.

Because I knew the fence wasn't a priority for the Obama administration, in July 2009 I offered an amendment to the DHS spending bill to force the president to finish the fence by the end of 2010. It passed easily with *21 Democrats supporting it.*

Under pressure from the White House, however, Democrat leaders stripped my amendment out of the bill behind closed doors, during negotiations between the Senate and the House.

Virtual vs. Layered Fencing

Those who oppose the double-layer fence promise Americans a "virtual fence" would best secure the border, which is where border security funds have been targeted in recent years instead of a real fence.

In 2007, our current DHS Secretary Janet Napolitano, then Democratic governor of Arizona, gave a speech at the National Press Club and boasted about the capabilities of a virtual fence. "We can shore up our border gaps with ground-based sensors, radar and unmanned aerial vehicles," she said. "Any combination of the above will work far better than any 10 or 20 or 50 miles of wall."

She was wrong.

A pair of reports published in late 2009 and early 2010 from the GAO proved virtual fencing is a virtual disaster. The GAO found [U.S.] Border Patrol agents were relying on cameras that suffered signal loss and that the number of new defects identified with the virtual fence outpaced the number that were being fixed. U.S. Customs and Border Protection chief Alan Bersin dashed any hopes left for the virtual fence when he called it a "complete failure" during a Senate hearing last month [April 2010].

Yet, we know layered fencing is effective. Layered-fence construction began in San Diego in 1996 and the Congressional Research Service found illegal apprehensions "dropped rapidly" afterwards. In 1996, the San Diego sector reported 480,000 illegal apprehensions. Apprehensions plummeted to 100,000 in 2002.

A Lack of Border Security

While Washington drags its feet on real border security, the consequences of the federal inaction are all too real. Drug trafficking, human trafficking, gang activity and other crimes are raging in American cities near the border.

The fence is a critical step, and only when the border is truly secure will Americans trust Washington to pass reform to create a legal immigration system that works.

Phoenix had 316 kidnapping cases last year, more than any other town in America, and nearly all of them involving illegal immigrants and drugs. Arizona's new governor, Republican Jan Brewer, wrote a letter to President Obama in April pleading for tougher enforcement. "This emergency has been the result of decades of neglect and an ongoing unwillingness by the federal government to fully shoulder its constitutional duty to secure our country's southern border with Mexico," Brewer said.

Brewer signed a law to crack down on illegal immigration later that month, which Obama misrepresented at a public event in Iowa. "If you don't have your papers and you took your kid out to get ice cream, you're going to be harassed," he said. This is untrue. The Arizona law specifically bans racial profiling and only allows inquiry into citizenship status if the person is stopped for some other crime.

As president, Obama's first priority should be protecting our citizens, not pandering to a liberal media with false attacks. Our nation's borders are fundamental to our national security and sovereignty. Americans shouldn't be forced to live under the threat of rising kidnapping, drug violence, and gang activity because of political posturing in Washington.

We all know that the fence alone will not solve the problem of illegal immigration, as we must also have interior enforcement of our immigration laws. But the fence is a critical step, and only when the border is truly secure will Americans trust Washington to pass reform to create a legal immigration system that works. That's why I will continue to fight for a vote on my "Finish the Fence Act" and force the federal government to keep its promise to the American people for real border security.

It's time to end the rhetoric, and finish the fence.

Congress Should End Birthright Citizenship

Will Wilkinson

Will Wilkinson is a research fellow at the Cato Institute and editor of Cato Unbound.

Even as Arizona continues to distinguish itself as America's undisputed leader in harebrained xenophobia, the state has stumbled upon a very good idea. Hot on the heels of SB 1070, the controversial Arizona law that hands cops expansive powers to detain anybody who gives off an insufficiently American vibe, Republican lawmakers in the state have set their sights on a new state law to deny citizenship to babies born on American soil whose parents lack proper papers.

Currently, anyone born within U.S. boundaries counts as a U.S. citizen, and it doesn't matter a bit how mom got in. The proposal to end "birthright citizenship" for the children of unauthorized immigrants springs from less than generous motives, and almost surely runs afoul of the U.S. Constitution. But ending it altogether is a better idea than you might think. (And if you already think it's a good idea, it's good for reasons you might find surprising.) For one, it would likely achieve the opposite of its intended result by making America more, rather than less, welcoming to newcomers.

The Need for a Common Labor Market

Well-ordered societies are extended networks of peaceful and productive cooperation, and those networks don't suddenly stop at political borderlines drawn by conquest and colonization. Americans and Mexicans are deeply intertwined by blood, soil, travel, toil and trade. After all, Arizona was Mexico once upon a time, until the U.S. seized Northwest Mexico and pushed the border south. Efforts to arbitrarily segregate people tied by history, culture, and mutual economic interest are bound to fail. The draconian Arizona model of immigration reform seeks to complete the colonizing work of Manifest Destiny by instituting a more perfect apartheid. It seeks to address the perception of a breakdown in the rule of law by ignoring causes in favor of aggressively treating symptoms. Higher walls. More guards, more guns, more jails. Your papers, please.

The alternative is to secure a peaceful and humane order through policies that acknowledge the cultural, economic, and geographical unity of northern Mexico and the American Southwest. The rule of law demands a clear set of equitable rules that respects and regulates natural patterns of traffic, that sets and sustains long-term expectations, and that facilitates and channels the fundamental human inclination to seek out opportunity and the benefits of cooperation. To set up a stop sign every five feet and then to crack down on people who don't follow the rules misses the point. So does establishing an imaginary line that restricts trade and travel while making a muddle of citizenship.

Birthright citizenship made sense for a frontier country with open borders; newly freed slaves; and a small, remote bureaucracy.

Fortunately, we already have a model of sensible reform from a frequently insensible place—the European Union [EU]. By establishing a common labor market in which Americans and Mexicans (Canadians too!) may range freely, living and working where they please, we can channel the commercial energy of integration while maintaining distinctly separate citizenship. Indeed, the feasibility of this arrangement requires maintaining a clear distinction between the right to live and work in another country's territory and the right to the benefits enjoyed by its citizens. It is a fact of modern life that the redistributive nation-state offers all manner of goods to citizens. To be a citizen of a wealthy country is a lot like being a member of a private club. Yet even the wealthiest national clubs are straining to deliver the benefits promised to members. If a club's rules permit visitors, invited or not, to mint new members simply by giving birth, cash-strapped current members are bound to object.

The EU's shortcomings, from bureaucratic micromanagement to a floundering common currency, have obscured its great practical and moral triumph: the dramatic expansion of European mobility rights and the inspiring integration of the continent's labor markets. When Britain opened its labor markets to Polish workers in 2004, the gap in average income between the two countries was about as big as that between the United States and Mexico. But per capita GDP [gross domestic product] in Poland has improved markedly since then, hastening the day when Poland provides a robust market for British goods—and possibly British labor, too. Similarly, by 2012, Romanians and Bulgarians, who are on average poorer than Mexicans, will be able to live and work in rich countries such as France, Germany, and Britain. It's worth noting, however, that not a single EU country has a birthright citizenship rule like that in the U.S.

Ending Birthright Citizenship

Birthright citizenship made sense for a frontier country with open borders; newly freed slaves; and a small, remote bureaucracy. But the time seems ripe to consider alternatives. Ending full birthright citizenship leaves open many intermediate possibilities, such as granting citizenship to children born to foreign citizens who have legally resided in the country for a predetermined number of years. In response to agitation over a growing population of Turkish guest workers, Germany changed its rules to grant citizenship to Germany-born children of Germany-born children of resident foreigners.

There's ample reason to believe a change in policy could make America a more immigrant-friendly place while simultaneously restricting the costly benefits of citizenship. Though undocumented immigrants are ineligible for most forms of government assistance, their America-born kids do qualify, which is no doubt an attraction to some prospective immigrant parents. The hard-right Arizona State Sen. Russell Pearce speaks for many Americans when he says birthright citizenship "rewards lawbreakers." What's more, because these children, once grown, can sponsor family members for authorized migration, they function as border-spanning bridges over which a retinue of relatives may trod. These relatives, once naturalized, can in turn sponsor aunts and uncles and cousins without end. Hence the fear of the "anchor baby," a gurgling demographic land mine set to explode into a multiheaded invasion of Telemundo fans.

Any move to thwart birthright citizenship will require a constitutional amendment.

The Need for a Constitutional Amendment

This line of thinking may be ugly, but there is no doubt that many Americans subscribe to it. According to Rasmussen Reports, 58 percent of Americans oppose birthright citizenship for kids of undocumented immigrants. However, those who wish to be rid of birthright citizenship—whether to hasten the freedom-enhancing arrival of a pan-American labor market (like me) or to put an end to the imagined scourge of anchor babies (like Sen. Pearce)—face a truly formidable obstacle: the 14th Amendment of the U.S. Constitution.

"All persons born or naturalized in the United States, and subject to the jurisdiction thereof, are citizens of the United

States and of the State wherein they reside," states the first sentence of the 1868 amendment. Long-standing precedent has established that the immigration status of the mother is usually irrelevant to the child's qualification for full membership in Club America. Arizona's Pearce, who promoted the state's vile SB 1070, argues that the 14th Amendment "was not intended for illegal aliens." But his constitutional case is hopeless. There were no "illegal aliens" in 1868. Back then, lawful residence in the U.S. merely required stepping over the border or onto the shore. Pearce's argument won't fly in court.

Consequently, any move to thwart birthright citizenship will require a constitutional amendment. So let's get to work! It's a big task, and if it's going to happen, it's going to require the cooperation of unlikely allies. Russell Pearce, call me.

Birthright Citizenship Should Not Be Eliminated

Margaret Stock

Margaret Stock is a retired military officer and an attorney who teaches in the Department of Political Science at the University of Alaska, Anchorage.

No one doubts the dysfunction of the current US immigration system, a dysfunction that has resulted in the presence in America of millions of illegal or unauthorized immigrants. Some have suggested that one partial "solution" to the problem of illegal immigration is to reinterpret or amend the Fourteenth Amendment to the US Constitution to eliminate birthright citizenship. Those who suggest this change argue that giving automatic American citizenship to persons born within the geographic limits of the United States encourages foreigners to enter or remain in the United States illegally. They refer pejoratively to "anchor babies," children born in the United States who are birthright citizens and who have parents who are not authorized to be here. They believe that children who gain citizenship by birth in the US serve to "anchor" their parents, because when the children turn 21, the parents can sometimes migrate legally based on their adult child's status as a citizen. This "anchor," they say, should be eliminated.

Yet, such a change would be ill-advised from a policy perspective.

US Citizenship Law

Legal scholars refer to the concept of birthright citizenship as "jus soli," the law of the soil, and the United States has had some form of this rule since the dawn of the Republic, although the concept was only enshrined in the US Constitution after the Civil War. Of course, there are other ways that one can become a United States citizen besides having the fortune of being born here—one can also derive citizenship through one's parent or parents ("jus sanguinis," or the law of blood) or obtain citizenship by applying for it through the naturalization process, usually after having first obtained "lawful permanent residence" first. Thus, if birthright citizenship is eliminated, many people born in the United States would still be American citizens by inheritance or could perhaps become citizens by filing an application for naturalization. Others, however, would not be eligible for derivative citizenship and would have no status allowing them to apply for American citizenship. They would remain "foreign denizens" resident here—at least until they legalized, left, or were deported.

Unfortunately, US law with regard to derivative citizenship is extremely complex. In fact, with the *exception* of the current birthright citizenship presumption, all of US immigration and nationality law is tremendously complicated, such that many people in the world who are US citizens—and many of their lawyers—do not know that they are citizens, or if they know, have trouble getting documents proving that they are. Immigrating legally to the United States is also a process of great difficulty and complexity, and unattainable by most.

It is also true that many native-born (birthright citizens) have trouble proving their citizenship. The United States has no national register of its birthright citizens; documents evidencing birth in America are created by thousands of state and local governmental entities as well as the Department of Homeland Security and the Department of State. Because the fact of birth in the United States has been the rule for hundreds of years, however, many Americans do not routinely obtain any governmental documents evidencing their citizenship status. A recent survey by the Brennan Center [for Justice] at New York University [School of Law] found that more than 13 million American adults cannot easily produce documentation proving their citizenship. But at least birthright citizenship can be proved by producing a valid US birth certificate, something that most birthright citizens can obtain without too much expense or difficulty if they are forced to do so.

US law with regard to derivative citizenship is extremely complex.

The Alternative to Birthright Citizenship

If birthright citizenship is eliminated, however, those born in the United States will lose their access to easy proof of citizenship. Instead, they will find it necessary to turn to the exceptionally complex US rules for citizenship by blood (the majority will be unable to qualify for the immigration visas necessary as a prerequisite to citizenship by naturalization). Yet the rules for derivative citizenship are so complicated that it can take an experienced immigration attorney more than an hour to determine conclusively whether someone is an American citizen by derivation—the lawyer must inquire about grandparents as well as parents, about marriage dates and birth dates of ancestors, and about the time that one's parents or grandparents spent in the United States prior to one's birth. In some cases, whether one's parents were married or unmarried at the time of one's birth makes a difference. Whether one's United States citizen parent was male or female also can be crucial to the determination (as a result of the US Supreme Court's decision in *Nguyen v. Reno*, the children of American men cannot claim US citizenship as easily as the children of American women).

Over more than two hundred years of American history, Congress has been responsible for creating the "jus sanguinis" rules in America, and Congress has made them so complicated that figuring out whether someone is a US citizen by blood is sometimes the equivalent of figuring out whether a patent application is valid. So, if we rid ourselves of the birthright citizenship presumption, what we will be doing is replacing a simple rule for most people with one that will be tremendously complex, as our current jus sanguinis rule is.

Under the birthright citizenship presumption in effect today, most Americans—but not all—have it much easier than the minority who are derivative citizens. Most Americans are presumed to be citizens by virtue of birth here. All they have to do to prove citizenship is produce a valid birth certificate. Were they not so presumed—and the hundreds of thousands of Americans born ... overseas do not have the benefit of such a presumption—a complex and individualized assessment of their status is required.

There are many such Americans born every year—the children of military members deployed overseas, missionaries, oil company employees, or Americans who choose to have their children in another country while visiting there. The State Department and the Department of Homeland Security [DHS] charge substantial fees to make derivative citizenship assessments (the current DHS fee is $457)—and depending on the facts, the assessment can take weeks, and require production of numerous documents, including very old historical records. The government also frequently makes mistakes with regard to people who have not undergone this assessment; any experienced immigration lawyer has stories of US citizen clients who have been deported—mistaken deportations of US citizens are relatively common.

A Good Rule

So what would it mean to eliminate birthright citizenship, as a practical matter? The United States has no national registry of

American citizens. Presumably, we would have to create one. Each person born in America—at thousands of localities, hospitals, midwiferies—would have to have his or her citizenship adjudicated. Someone expert would have to do the adjudication—most probably a trained immigration attorney—unless we allow these complex adjudications to be made randomly by bureaucrats. Finding such attorneys is very difficult today, but will likely become even more difficult, in that immigration and citizenship law is a field that a Department of Homeland Security spokesperson has accurately called "a mystery and a mastery of obfuscation."

As a practical matter, the elites of American society are unlikely to be affected much by this. A change in the current system will cause little trouble for those who have the money to hire highly trained lawyers to handle their paperwork. The burden of proving citizenship is likely to fall mostly on the less favored elements in society. As mentioned above, one of the little-known facts of US immigration law is that the US government frequently deports US citizens—but those US citizens who get deported are mostly the less favored in our society—the poor, the uneducated, the mentally disturbed, and minorities. This trend will accelerate if we eliminate birthright citizenship.

> *If birthright citizenship is eliminated ... those born in the United States will lose their access to easy proof of citizenship.*

So the first policy argument against eliminating birthright citizenship is this: We have a clear, long-standing rule of citizenship law—one that is easy to understand and easy to administer. It is also a constitutional rule. This rule has been in effect, de facto, since the dawn of the Republic, and by constitutional law since the end of the Civil War. Those who would overturn or change this rule have the burden of proving why this rule should be changed, as a matter of policy and not just as a matter of law. This rule is much easier to administer than other rules like jus sanguinis (the rule of citizenship by blood). Everyone should appreciate long-standing, easy to use, "bright line" rules. To date, advocates of change have not made the policy case for why the long-standing rule should be changed.

The Arguments for Ending Birthright Citizenship

The test of any public policy is whether the benefits of the policy are likely to outweigh the costs. Here, there is no question that proponents of changing the current default rule have not made even a marginal case on policy grounds. They cite vague policy reasons for changing the law such as the need to make US citizenship more valuable; the need to stop what they term an "industry" of women coming to the US to have babies. They seem to assume, without benefit of any hard data, that the US does not benefit from birthright citizenship. And yet there is ample evidence that it does; hundreds of thousands of birthright citizens make tremendous contributions to American society every day, serving in our military, in public office—Senator Pete Domenici, the most famous anchor baby in America, is one example. Opponents of birthright citizenship also assume—again without data—that illegal immigration will lessen or even stop if birthright citizenship is eliminated. Although there may be some people who might be deterred from coming to the US if birthright citizenship is eliminated, instead of reducing the number of illegal migrants within our borders, changing the current rule will make even more people into illegal migrants. We know from the European and Asian experiences with jus sanguinis rules that eliminating jus soli does not stop illegal immigration, but does increase the number of illegal aliens within a country, because fewer people are able to gain legal status.

The number of US-born children of illegal immigrants is estimated to be 3 million—but nobody really has a good idea how many there actually are. And yet facts are critically necessary to evaluate the efficacy of any seismic change to the birthright citizenship rule. Some 200,000–400,000 "anchor babies" are believed to be born each year, but there's no real way to track it because hospitals in America don't report the citizenship status of parents when children are born. They do report—without verification—what the parents self-report as the birthplace of the parents—but a parent's birthplace tells nothing about the parent's citizenship status. And yet without any hard data, or proof that a change in policy will achieve the policy goals sought by the change, proponents of a change want to cause tremendous hardship and expense to all the rest of America.

The Consequences of Ending Birthright Citizenship

While opponents of birthright citizenship seem to assume without facts that their rule will do some good, we do have a pretty good idea what bad things will happen if we eliminate the birthright citizenship rule:

First, we will have thousands of children born every year who have no citizenship. To cite just one group, under the pending congressional legislation, children of asylees and refugees will have no citizenship. They will be left without a country, creating an underclass of "exploitable denizens." This is what has happened in countries—like France—that do not have a jus soli ("common law") rule.

Second, the benefit does not seem to outweigh the cost. Why not just take the money we'd use to adjudicate the citizenship status of 300 million Americans and use it to enforce existing immigration laws?

Third, eliminating birthright citizenship is un-American. This is our unique heritage, one that hundreds of thousands of soldiers—citizens and noncitizens—fought the Civil War to enforce. Birthright citizenship has been the rule since the dawn of the Republic, and we ought to have a pretty good reason to change it—one better than some frustration with the federal government's inability to enforce existing immigration law. Further, what we are really talking about here is punishing children for something "bad" that their parents did—or maybe not even anything bad but just being from the wrong country.

We have a clear, long-standing rule of citizenship law—one that is easy to understand and easy to administer.

Finally, changing our rule would cause us to contribute heavily to the current global population of stateless people. And we as a nation have professed that people have a human right to have a country.

In sum, the policy arguments in favor of retaining birthright citizenship as a rule are very, very strong. The policy arguments against it are weak. Even if we believe that it is possible to interpret the Fourteenth Amendment differently than we have been interpreting it for more than a hundred years, it's not clear why we would want to do so. Trading an easy and egalitarian birthright citizenship rule for one that will cause hardship to millions of Americans is not a smart way to solve our complex immigration problems.

Organizations to Contact

The editors have compiled the following list of organizations concerned with the issues debated in this book. The descriptions are derived from materials provided by the organizations. All have publications or information available for interested readers. The list was compiled on the date of publication of the present volume; the information provided here may change. Be aware that many organizations take several weeks or longer to respond to inquiries, so allow as much time as possible.

American Civil Liberties Union (ACLU)
125 Broad Street, 18th Floor, New York, NY   10004
(212) 549-2500
e-mail: infoaclu@aclu.org
website: www.aclu.org

The American Civil Liberties Union (ACLU) is a national organization that works to defend Americans' civil rights as guaranteed in the US Constitution. Its Immigrants' Rights Project is dedicated to expanding and enforcing the civil liberties and civil rights of noncitizens, and to combating public and private discrimination against immigrants. The ACLU publishes the semiannual newsletter *Civil Liberties Alert* as well as briefing papers, including the publication "Immigration Myths and Facts."

American Immigration Council
1331 G Street NW, Suite 200, Washington, DC   20005-3141
(202) 507-7500 • fax: (202) 742-5619
website: www.americanimmigrationcouncil.org

The American Immigration Council (formerly the American Immigration Law Foundation) is an educational organization that works to strengthen America by honoring its immigrant history. The American Immigration Council promotes humane immigration policies that honor human rights and works to achieve fairness for immigrants under the law. It publishes numerous fact sheets and reports through its Immigration Policy Center, including "The Economic Blame Game: U.S. Unemployment Is Not Caused by Immigration."

Americans for Immigration Control (AIC)
PO Box 738, Monterey, VA   24465
(540) 468-2023 • fax: (540) 468-2026
e-mail: aic@immigrationcontrol.com
website: www.immigrationcontrol.com

Americans for Immigration Control (AIC) is a nonpartisan organization that favors deportation of illegal immigrants and opposes amnesty and guest worker legislation. AIC works to educate and motivate citizens to join efforts to secure America's borders. AIC publishes several books, videos, and reports on the topic of immigration, including "Amnesty for Illegal Immigrants: A Policy of False Compassion."

Cato Institute
1000 Massachusetts Avenue NW
Washington, DC   20001-5403
(202) 842-0200 • fax: (202) 842-3490
website: www. cato.org

The Cato Institute is a public policy research foundation dedicated to limiting the role of government, protecting individual liberties, and promoting free markets. The institute commissions a variety of publications including books, monographs, briefing papers, and other studies. Among its publications are the quarterly magazine *Regulation*, the bimonthly *Cato Policy Report*, and the monthly *Immigration Reform Bulletin*.

Center for Immigration Studies (CIS)
1522 K Street NW, Suite 820, Washington, DC   20005-1202
(202) 466-8185 • fax: (202) 466-8076
e-mail: center@cis.org
website: www.cis.org

The Center for Immigration Studies (CIS) is an independent research organization devoted exclusively to research and policy analysis of the economic, social, demographic, fiscal, and other impacts of immigration on the United States. The Center for Immigration Studies is animated by a unique pro-immigrant, low-immigration vision that seeks fewer immigrants but a warmer welcome for those admitted. The Center for Immigration Studies publishes reports, memos, and opinion pieces available at its website, including "Is the U.S. Immigration Debate Going in the Right Direction?"

Federation for American Immigration Reform (FAIR)
25 Massachusetts Avenue NW, Suite 330
Washington, DC   20001
(202) 328-7004 • fax: (202) 387-3447
e-mail: comments@fairus.org
website: www.fairus.org

The Federation for American Immigration Reform (FAIR) is a nonprofit organization of concerned citizens who share a common belief that the nation's immigration policies must be reformed to serve the national interest. FAIR seeks to improve border security, to stop illegal immigration, and to promote immigration levels at rates of about three hundred thousand a year. FAIR publishes the monthly *Immigration Report* and other publications, including "Amnesty and Joblessness: Unemployed Americans Shouldn't Have to Compete for Jobs with Illegal Aliens."

Migration Policy Institute (MPI)
1400 Sixteenth Street NW, Suite 300, Washington, DC   20036
(202) 266-1940 • fax: (202) 266-1900
e-mail: info@migrationpolicy.org
website: www.migrationpolicy.org

The Migration Policy Institute (MPI) is an independent, nonpartisan think tank dedicated to the study of the movement of people worldwide. MPI provides analysis, development, and evaluation of migration and refugee policies at the local, national, and international levels. MPI publishes books, reports, fact sheets, and policy briefs, including "Earned Legalization: Effects of Proposed Requirements on Unauthorized Men, Women, and Children."

National Council of La Raza (NCLR)
Raul Yzaguirre Bldg., 1126 Sixteenth Street NW, Suite 600, Washington, DC 20036-4845
(202) 785-1670 • fax: (202) 776-1792
e-mail: comments@nclr.org
website: www.nclr.org

The National Council of La Raza (NCLR) is a national organization that promotes civil rights and economic opportunities for Hispanics. NCLR conducts immigration policy analyses and advocacy activities in its role as a civil rights organization. NCLR publishes a quarterly newsletter *Agenda*, as well as reports and briefs, including "The Impact of Section 287(g) of the Immigration and Nationality Act on the Latino Community."

National Immigration Forum
50 F Street NW, Suite 300, Washington, DC 20001
(202) 347-0040 • fax: (202) 347-0058
website: www.immigrationforum.org

The National Immigration Forum is an organization that advocates for the value of immigrants and immigration to the nation. The National Immigration Forum works to foster immigration policy that honors American ideals, protects human dignity, reflects the economic demands of the United States, celebrates family unity, and provides opportunities for progress. The forum publishes numerous backgrounders, fact sheets, and issue papers, including "Assets or Enemies: Securing Our Nation by Enforcing Immigration Laws."

National Immigration Law Center (NILC)
3435 Wilshire Boulevard, Suite 2850, Los Angeles, CA 90010
(213) 639-3900 • fax: (213) 639-3911

e-mail: info@nilc.org
website: www.nilc.org

The National Immigration Law Center (NILC) is dedicated to protecting and promoting the rights of low-income immigrants and their family members. NILC engages in policy advocacy, impact litigation, and education to secure fair treatment in the courts for immigrants, preserve a safety net for immigrants, and open opportunities for immigrants. NILC publishes manuals and analyses for nonprofit agencies working on immigration issues, including *Immigrants' Rights Update*, a newsletter focused on changes in policy, legislation, and case law affecting low-income immigrants.

National Network for Immigrant and Refugee Rights (NNIRR)

310 Eighth Street, Suite 303, Oakland, CA   94607
(510) 465-1984 • fax: (510) 465-1885
e-mail: nnirr@nnirr.org
website: www.nnirr.org

The National Network for Immigrant and Refugee Rights (NNIRR) is a national organization that serves as a forum to share information and analysis, to educate communities and the general public, and to develop and coordinate plans of action on important immigrant and refugee issues. NNIRR works to promote a just immigration and refugee policy in the United States, and to defend and expand the rights of all immigrants and refugees, regardless of immigration status. NNIRR publishes fact sheets and reports, including "Injustice for All: The Rise of the U.S. Immigration Policing Regime."

Negative Population Growth (NPG)

2861 Duke Street, Suite 36, Alexandria, VA   22314
(703) 370-9510 • fax: (703) 370-9514
e-mail: npg@npg.org
website: www.npg.org

Negative Population Growth (NPG) is a membership organization that aims to educate the American public and political leaders about the detrimental effects of overpopulation on the environment, resources, and quality of life. NPG advocates for a smaller and sustainable US population accomplished through smaller families and lower, more traditional immigration levels. NPG publishes a quarterly newsletter, *Population Perspectives*, and numerous reports, position papers, and fact sheets, among which is "The Great Silence: U.S. Population Policy."

NumbersUSA
1601 N Kent Street, Suite 1100, Arlington, VA   22209
(703) 816-8820
website: www.numbersusa.com

NumbersUSA is a nonprofit, nonpartisan public policy organization that favors an environmentally sustainable and economically just America. NumbersUSA opposes efforts to use federal immigration policies to force mass US population growth and to depress wages of vulnerable workers. Numbers-USA publishes fact sheets, including "High Immigration = Bigger Government."

US Citizenship and Immigration Services (USCIS)
425 I Street NW, Washington, DC   20536
(800) 375-5283
website: www.uscis.gov

US Citizenship and Immigration Services (USCIS) is the government agency that oversees lawful immigration to the United States. USCIS provides immigration information, grants immigration and citizenship benefits, promotes an awareness and understanding of citizenship, and ensures the integrity of the US immigration system. USCIS provides numerous reports, informational resources, and immigration forms.

US Immigration and Customs Enforcement (ICE)
500 Twelfth Street SW, Washington, DC   20536
(202) 732-4242
website: www.ice.gov

The US Immigration and Customs Enforcement (ICE) is the largest investigative agency in the US Department of Homeland Security (DHS). ICE's mission is to protect the security of the American people and homeland by vigilantly enforcing the nation's immigration and customs laws. ICE publishes the quarterly *Cornerstone Report*, fact sheets, and reports.

Bibliography

Books

Darrell Ankarlo	*Illegals: The Unacceptable Cost of America's Failure to Control Its Borders*. Nashville, TN: Thomas Nelson, 2010.
David Bacon	*Illegal People: How Globalization Creates Migration and Criminalizes Immigrants*. Boston: Beacon Press, 2008.
Justin Akers Chacón and Mike Davis	*No One Is Illegal: Fighting Violence and State Repression on the US-Mexico Border*. Chicago: Haymarket Books, 2006.
Aviva Chomsky	*"They Take Our Jobs!": And 20 Other Myths About Immigration*. Boston: Beacon Press, 2007.
Jane Guskin and David L. Wilson	*The Politics of Immigration: Questions and Answers*. New York: Monthly Review Press, 2007.
J.D. Hayworth	*Whatever It Takes: Illegal Immigration, Border Security, and the War on Terror*. Washington, DC: Regnery, 2006.
Bill Ong Hing	*Deporting Our Souls: Values, Morality, and Immigration Policy*. New York: Cambridge University Press, 2006.

James K.
Hoffmeier

The Immigration Crisis: Immigrants, Aliens, and the Bible. Wheaton, IL: Crossway Books, 2009.

Kevin R. Johnson

Opening the Floodgates: Why America Needs to Rethink Its Borders and Immigration Laws. New York: New York University Press, 2007.

Mark Krikorian

The New Case Against Immigration: Both Legal and Illegal. New York: Sentinel, 2008.

Heather
MacDonald,
Victor Davis
Hanson, and
Steven Malanga

The Immigration Solution: A Better Plan than Today's. Chicago: Ivan R. Dee, 2007.

Nicolaus Mills,
ed.

Arguing Immigration: The Debate over the Changing Face of America. New York: Simon & Schuster, 2007.

Lina Newton

Illegal, Alien, or Immigrant: The Politics of Immigration Reform. New York: New York University Press, 2008.

Jason L. Riley

Let Them In: The Case for Open Borders. New York: Gotham Books, 2008.

Peter Schrag

Not Fit for Our Society: Immigration and Nativism in America. Berkeley: University of California Press, 2010.

Carol M. Swain,
ed.

Debating Immigration. New York: Cambridge University Press, 2007.

Tom Tancredo *In Mortal Danger: The Battle for America's Border and Security.* Nashville, TN: WND Books, 2006.

Helen Thorpe *Just Like Us: The True Story of Four Mexican Girls Coming of Age in America.* New York: Scribner, 2009.

Periodicals and Internet Sources

Sasha Abramsky "Gimme Shelter," *Nation*, February 25, 2008.

America "Migration, the Larger Picture," January 7, 2008.

David Bacon "Railroading Immigrants," *Nation*, September 17, 2008.

Michael Barone "Why Enforcement Matters," *US News & World Report*, June 4, 2007.

George R. Boggs "Why Congress Should Revive the Dream Act," *Chronicle of Higher Education*, March 28, 2008.

William F. Buckley Jr. "Illegalizing Illegals," *National Review*, November 3, 2007.

California Immigrant Policy Center "Immigrants and the U.S. Health Care System," January 2007. www.caimmigrant.org.

Steven A. Camarota "Immigration, Both Legal and Illegal, Puts Huge Strain on the Country," *North County Times* (CA), December 15, 2007.

Megan Eckstein
"In-State Tuition for Undocumented Students: Not Quite Yet," *Chronicle of Higher Education*, May 8, 2009.

Economist
"Not Very NICE," April 24, 2008.

Federation for American Immigration Reform (FAIR)
"Illegal Immigration and Public Health," 2009. www.fairus.org.

Marshall Fitz and Angela Maria Kelley
"Principles for Immigration Reform: Guidelines for Fixing Our Broken Immigration System," Center for American Progress, December 21, 2009. www.americanprogress.org.

Lino A. Graglia
"Birthright Citizenship for Children of Illegal Aliens: An Irrational Public Policy," *Texas Review of Law & Politics*, vol. 14, Fall 2009.

Alan Greenblatt
"Immigration Debate," *CQ Researcher*, February 1, 2008.

Larry Greenley
"How to Fix Illegal Immigration," *New American*, March 3, 2008.

Daniel Griswold
"Comprehensive Immigration Reform: Finally Getting It Right," *Free Trade Bulletin*, May 16, 2007.

Jim Harper
"Electronic Employment Eligibility Verification: Franz Kafka's Solution to Illegal Immigration," *Policy Analysis*, March 6, 2008.

Greg Hirshman
"Protect Our Border: Build a Fence," *Stanford Review*, June 11, 2008.

Immigrants' Rights Project
"Prolonged Immigration Detention of Individuals Who Are Challenging Removal," *ACLU IRP Issue Brief*, July 2009. www.aclu.org.

John Judis
"Phantom Menace: The Psychology Behind America's Immigration Hysteria," *New Republic*, February 13, 2008.

John F. Kavanaugh
"Amnesty? Let Us Be Vigilant and Charitable," *America*, March 10, 2008.

Tom Knott
"Dream Act Begins an American Nightmare," *Washington Times*, October 11, 2007.

Kris Kobach
"A Sleeper Amnesty: Time to Wake Up from the DREAM Act," Backgrounder, no. 2069, September 13, 2007. www.heritage.org.

Edward Koch
"Imprisoned Illegal Aliens Should Be Deported," Newsmax, August 31, 2009. www.newsmax.com.

Mark Krikorian
"No Amnesty—Now or in Two Years," *National Review Online*, October 31, 2008. www.nationalreview.com.

Elena Lacayo
"The Impact of Section 287(G) of the Immigration and Nationality Act on the Latino Community," National Council of La Raza, *Issue Brief*, 2010. www.nclr.org.

Steven Malanga
"Illegal in More Ways than One," *City Journal*, Spring 2008.

John F. McManus "The Battle Against Illegal Immigration," *New American*, March 3, 2008.

Jena Baker McNeill "Amnesty as an Economic Stimulus: Not the Answer to the Illegal Immigration Problem," WebMemo, no. 2451, May 18, 2009. www.heritage.org.

Stephanie Mencimer "Why Texas Still Holds 'em," *Mother Jones*, July/August 2008.

Melissa Merrell "The Impact of Unauthorized Immigrants on the Budgets of State and Local Governments," Congressional Budget Office, December 2007.

Jason Richwine "A Population Portrait: Who Illegal Immigrants Are, and What They Bring with Them," *National Review Online*, June 7, 2010. www.nationalreview.com.

Rubén G. Rumbaut and Walter A. Ewing "The Myth of Immigrant Criminality and the Paradox of Assimilation: Incarceration Rates Among Native and Foreign-Born Men," Immigration Policy Center, Spring 2007. www.immigrationpolicy.org.

Charles Scaliger "Avoiding Extreme Solutions," *New American*, March 4, 2008.

Peter Schrag "Divided States," *Nation*, January 7, 2008.

Emma Schwartz   "A Bust, and a Blow to a Business,"
                US News & World Report, October 1,
                2007.

Beth   "Held in Purgatory," *Ms.*, Summer
Schwartzapfel   2009.

Geri Smith and "On the Border: The 'Virtual Fence'
Keith Epstein   Isn't Working," *BusinessWeek*,
                February 7, 2008.

Nathan   "Undocumented and Undeterred,"
Thornburgh   *Time*, April 27, 2009.

Washington Times   "End the Dream," October 24, 2007.

Darrell M. West "Seven Myths That Cloud
                 Immigration Debate," *USA Today*,
                 September 1, 2010.

Index

Unemployment
   education effects, 124, 139–
      140
   exacerbated by illegal immi-
      gration, 82–85, 134–140
   need to decrease benefits,
      84–85
   rise for illegals, 105
   See also Employment consid-
      erations
University education for illegal
   immigrants, 122–129
U.S. Border Patrol
   apprehensions usually nonvio-
      lent, 89–90
   not enforcing penalties, 26
   reports on increased crossings,
      40
   virtual fencing defects, 142
U.S. Chamber of Commerce, 40
U.S. Citizenship and Immigration
   Service (CIS), 28, 99
U.S. Congress
   American opinions on illegal
      immigration, 27
   history of immigration policy,
      96–100
   immigration reform legisla-
      tion, 39–41, 42, 134, 136
   testimony on crime, 50
U.S. Constitution, 14th Amendment, 122, 148–149, 150, 157
U.S. Customs and Border Protection (CBP), 15, 100
   See also U.S. Border Patrol
U.S. Department of Homeland
   Security (DHS)
   border fencing, 141, 142
   creation, 99
   derivative citizenship assess-
      ments, 153, 154

illegal immigrant numbers,
   14, 20, 83
See also 287(g) programs
U.S. Department of State, 153
U.S. Immigration and Customs
   Enforcement (ICE)
   Arizona bill requirements, 15
   creation, 100
   Criminal Alien Program, 112–
      113
   illegal immigrant detentions,
      25, 31
   tough enforcement actions of
      2005, 31
   See also 287(g) programs
U.S. Immigration and Naturalization Service (INS)
   crime rate estimates, 79
   mass removals of 1954, 30
   restructuring, 99–100
U.S.-Mexico border
   ease of crossing, 14, 26
   fencing, 141–144
   increased enforcement actions,
      30–31, 99
   smuggling and kidnapping
      operations, 90–91
U.S. Supreme Court, 122, 152
US-VISIT program, 105
USCIS (U.S. Citizenship and Immigration Service), 28, 99
Utah
   higher education for illegal
      immigrants, 128
   illegal immigrant population
      trends, 21

V

Vaughan, Jessica M., 107–116
Verification of legal status